D1503412

The Ghetto Game

Racial Conflicts in the City

The Ghetto Game

Racial Conflicts in the City

by Dennis Clark

SHEED AND WARD - New York

E184
.A1C53

Contents

The Ghetto Game

Racial Conflicts in the City

1

Race and Our Cities

IN THE COMING YEARS the United States will be reshaping its national life into social patterns dominated by the metropolis. The city of the atomic age with its strategic core, immense production and transportation systems, and its suburban hinterlands will in the future be the central feature of our national social life. It is calculated that by 1975 one hundred forty million people, or two thirds of the nation, will live in the major metropolitan areas alone, with much of the remaining population living in smaller cities.[1] In these metropolitan centers, where technology and population growth combine to produce a way of life novel in history, Americans will confront the social problems of a mass society in a new context. In this environment of the huge and exciting technical city, our citizens will again face the historic problem of racism, whose menacing shadow has stalked our democracy throughout the life of the American republic.

Racial difficulties have plagued our nation as a tragic doubt corrodes a great hope. The problems of racial discrimination and segregation have persisted despite the upheavals of war and the changes brought by tremendous social progress, as the panorama of our country's life changed from immigrant to native, from rural to urban and from a world position of isolated weakness to one of international leadership. The legacy of slavery and the tradition of racism have been to the United States what class hatreds and fratricidal nationalism have been to European countries. Race relations have been marked by violence, frustration and widespread suffering. Historically, they have been the central factor in a prolonged schism between the two oldest regions of the country. Legally and politically, the treatment of non-white groups has produced a web of anomalies and threatened the integrity of our constitutional commitment to the ideals of democratic humanism. Morally, the problem of race has mocked the power of religion in our national life. It is in the light of these facts that our citizens must now dispose themselves to deal with racial problems in the fluid and contradictory environment of the growing city.

The modern metropolis has gathered together people from a bewildering variety of cultures and backgrounds. Its sheer size has induced a constant exchange and migration of people who move to facilitate employment, education, achievement of social status or family improvement. The growth of our population and of the cities themselves has been rapid, but although this has been an important factor, the role of foreign immigration has been even more decisive in determining the relationships between population groups.[2]

The Immigrant Groups

The formation of the residential group was a response of newly arrived immigrants to the confusion and strangeness of the nineteenth-century city. This ethnic enclave based upon language difference or foreign origin became a fixture of American urban areas. It was a form of social protection and expression and a testimony to the pluralist character of our national life. Little Italy, Irishtown, Chinatown—dozens of such immigrant clusters dotted the cities. These neighborhoods provided the setting for the drama of ethnic group life. They also conditioned the common attitude and expectations with regard to the family and residential life of ethnic groups within the larger urban society. In the last century, the ethnic neighborhoods almost always established a picture in the public mind of poor living conditions and social disorganization. For over a century this picture was transmitted to a nation dominated by rural, native-born citizens, who prided themselves on their isolation from "foreign" influences and whose virtues of self-reliance and stability contrasted with the disorders of the struggling urban immigrant groups.

Eventually the dynamic quality of our urban life began to dissolve the ethnic communities which had partitioned the larger cities. Foreign immigration on a large scale ceased, and the influence of cultural media hastened the assimilation of the immigrant worlds which had flourished for decades. Physical and social mobility quickened this trend. But the experience of the immigration period and the concentration of ethnic groups had left a strong imprint upon national opinion. The stereotypes with regard to the attitudes and practices of ethnic groups were a part of the general cultural outlook. They did not dissipate as the ethnic communities themselves waned in significance, for they were consecrated by tradition. They were given wider currency and more vivid outlines by their use in the mass media which grew up to serve the urban populations.

In addition, the fluidity of urban society created a great hunger for social status. Distinctions based on ethnic and racial characteristics became important instruments in the psychic game of status seeking. Thus, although rising educational levels have reduced the crudity of the prejudices and stereotypes in-

herited from the American immigration experience, that experience was too sustained and significant not to leave lasting
impressions.

The persistence of racial and ethnic distinctions was helped
by the fact that leadership in the industrial metropolis was not
unitary but composed of a balance of contending groups re-
flecting the economic, ethnic and religious affiliations of the
citizens.[3] A wide diversity of leaders emerged in the political
and civil life of the urban areas. In some an oligarchy of "old
families" or political bosses became dominant, but their power
was always conditioned by the presence of the disparate representatives of a variety of groups. Under these conditions, it was
not wholly unnatural that racial groups should be set apart and
cultivated as were the other urban population elements grouped
around national origin, language or religion.

Metropolitan Change

At mid-twentieth century the American metropolis was still
in a rapidly changing state. The original traditions of civic life
and ideals were overlaid with decades of political-machine history and struggle with social change. In the expression and conduct of democratic civic and political life, the city was badly
compromised.[4] Political reforms and city reorganizations were
offset by the new problems created by mass populations. Improvements in government and education and the growth of
"the affluent society" had given the metropolis a more competent citizenry, but this citizenry was not dedicated to seeking
the general welfare. Social critics decried the apathy of the citizens and their studied indifference to the pressing problems of
metropolitan growth.

In terms of practical community responses to problems of urban change, the city and suburban populations were only dimly aware of the new metropolitan status that their environment had assumed. The coming of the automobile and the development of great suburban tracts of land had vastly broadened the urban centers. The resulting communities, however, were still firmly wedded to a traditional ideal of insulated community life. Local boroughs and townships looked upon proposals for co-operation and federation with deep suspicion.[5] The older cities, themselves within their outmoded boundaries, were far from united or purposeful in meeting the challenges of decay and transition. Racial partition within the cities and civic isolationism in the suburbs produced a situation in which the metropolis was fragmented. This fragmentation was all the more contradictory and confusing because of the technical and population forces which were dramatically enlarging the metropolis.[6]

Within this confusing situation there were sporadic cycles of urban renewal and social improvement. The concept of public planning and redevelopment under government auspices had gained wide acceptance. Wherever redevelopment took place, the subjects of community structure and population distribution were sure to arise. Where there were concentrations of racial groups, the movement to rebuild immediately presented the question of the disposition to be made of the ethnic communities. Cities cannot be rebuilt without moving people. People could not be moved without defying the ethnic taboos and racial codes of the past. As if the technical complexity of urban renewal were not enough, the city fathers were called upon to exercise social judgments that would have taxed the wisdom of Solomon. The ability to reshape communities physically did not bring with it a social wisdom that would promote the gentle fusion of antagonistic elements of the population.

Thus the rapidly changing metropolis of the 1950's, beset by a variety of vexing problems, was still hampered by the tradition of racial distinctions. These distinctions were endorsed by mass psychology, made concrete by discrimination and segregation practices and institutionalized in the racial grouping of population. Whereas most of the foreign-language and immigrant communities were being dissolved by mobile urban conditions, those racial groups which were identifiable by physical appearance were still subject to shrewdly enforced segregation and unequal treatment.[7] This took its most striking form in the stubborn residential segregation that has withstood the general movement of betterment in other areas of race relations.

In the metropolitan centers of our nation there has been considerable renovation of racial attitudes and a gradual abandonment of the more flagrant discriminatory practices aimed at people of color. The Second World War with the social changes it induced gave impetus to much of this improvement. Changes in the law and in the economic and educational standards of non-whites have also been influential. Public accommodations laws guaranteeing service in public places are now enforced, except in the South. Fair employment practices laws and the utilization of manpower without regard to race have brought some relief to minority groups. The active leadership of civil rights organizations and political parties has thrust race relations problems before the public. While race relations are far from satisfactory, there has been improvement. The outstanding exception lies in the field of housing and residential restrictions. Although better employment has permitted some improvement of housing conditions within the prevailing segregated residential situation, there has been little relaxation of the restrictive practices designed to contain racial groups within designated geographical areas.

Indeed the phenomenon of residential segregation has been magnified as a city problem by the great increases in the non-white urban population. By 1950 the cities held 62% of the nation's Negro population, most of it in the major cities. By 1960 this figure had risen to 66%.[8] Large numbers of other non-whites and a growing Puerto Rican population, which contained many persons who would be classified as non-whites, were spread throughout the cities. Practically all of the great increase of non-whites in the metropolitan areas in the last decade has been concentrated within the segregated residential districts. Originally these "ghettos" were merely ethnic enclaves on a par with a series of other ethnic concentrations. In the 1800's and in the early part of this century they were part of a system of urban ethnic "balkanization." Today these racial islands have expanded into continents, while their white ethnic counterparts have all but disappeared. The Negro areas have become something unique in their size and persistence. They are striking testimonies to the extension of racism right into the most advanced and active portions of American society.

The problem of racial discrimination and inequality in the United States has been inescapably bound up with the regional life and social history of the Southern states. Commentary and criticism about racial problems has largely had reference to the Southern context. As a national social issue the subject has been steadily attributed to the South and discussed in pejorative terms with respect to the South. This is no longer possible; the historic question has undergone an historic change. No development since the abolition of slavery has affected the problem to the same extent as has urbanization of hundreds of thousands of Negroes. The persistence of segregation through residential restrictions in the major cities of the nation has placed the racial issue in an entirely new social situation for the first time in a century.

Old Problem in New Form

The concentration of people of color in the "black belts" or urban centers has made a full-scale national phenomenon of a system of racial attitudes and restrictions which was formerly a regional condition peculiar to the South.[9] Segregated housing has brought segregation as a social institution into full play in the technical and industrial centers of the nation's strength. Not only is it impossible for the practical problems inherent in this development to be ignored, but the extension of large-scale segregation presents a test of all our democratic professions. While liberal and religious leaders have been leading campaigns to strike down racial restrictions in jobs, education and public services, massive segregation on a residential basis has proceeded almost without hindrance. This residential restriction by color has begotten other forms of racial discrimination. Community practices intended to insure, augment or facilitate residential segregation have affected employment, schools and the use of public facilities.[10] The gains won by the civil rights crusaders in forays against various selected targets have been counterbalanced by racial practices rooted in the system of housing segregation.

Massive segregation in urban centers is one of the characteristics of this mass society. In a social system where populations are vast and social movements huge and widespread, it is hardly possible to have segregation here and there on a small scale. Popular phenomena with roots deep in time simply do not occur in this manner in a mass society. Segregation is such a phenomenon, and its dimensions have been proportionate to the breadth of the urbanized mass society.

Ironically, the racial isolationism of the city neighborhood provides a refuge for the harried personality of the urbanite.[11]

Stripped of many of the protective affiliations of pre-industrial days, the urban man moves in an impersonal world. He works, eats and attends commercialized recreation and cultural functions in an impersonal and often starkly mechanized environment. The residential sphere, however, still has a somewhat personalized quality. In the home and its surroundings the city-dweller retains some emotional ties and intimate personal affiliations. Hence when the residential area is challenged by racial change, the last community bastion of personalized white sentiment is assaulted. Added to all the other emotionally potent features of racial reaction, this sense of ultimate social engagement heightens the intensity of the urban response to racial change in local life.

It is no doubt true also that popular generalizations and cynicism about racial groups is a response to the complex character and impersonality of mass social life. The city-dweller cannot take time out from his clockwatch and timetable existence of routines and disciplines to verify the facts behind racial stereotypes. Experiences and observations must be classified rather crudely for him. The pressure of popular opinion is great. So he accepts the canons of racial isolationism and alienation as part of the code of city living. This is the easy way out, which avoids all the complicated wrangles about anthropology and property values and minority rights. The simplified racial fictions are preferable to the complex truths to men who are surfeited with complexity.

Perhaps the greatest significance of this newer and nation-wide elaboration of racism through housing segregation is the fact that it has been associated with the most notable upsurge of urbanism that any country has ever experienced. In the last forty years the United States has become an urban nation in a most extraordinary sense of the word. The technology and energy of our people have created a wholly distinctive mode of urban living. Within the new cities a life of sufficiency, dignity and freedom is possible for millions. The old peasant world with its subjection of man to nature's whims has declined; the new urban society of high opportunity, mobility, and, for many, real affluence is expanding all around us. But there has been carried into this shining new world of urban comfort and control the ancient paradox of segregation. It is like a defiant, jerry-built old battlement among the graceful skyscrapers, frowning down on the cities.

The conjunction of residential segregation with our increasingly powerful urban development presents a grave quandary. We know that our era of urban expansion will be formative of the nation's social future. The social outlook and traditions of the metropolitan America ahead of us will be greatly affected by the policies we adopt today. Has our failure to abolish residential segregation already confirmed it as part of the metropolitan pattern for decades ahead? Have we already distilled reservoirs of civil discord and bitterness that will break upon the peace of our future cities? To what extent will residential segregation give a new lease on life to the waning ethnic antagonisms and racist excitements that have been such a peril to our pluralist society? The connection between housing segregation and the rise of the metropolis poses these questions for us.

The urban centers will experience many changes that will affect their ability to deal with racial questions. In the immediate future there will be wide changes in the age groups composing the population. The proportion of children and older persons will increase. Whether this will assist or retard racial understanding is problematical. Today American urban institutions are undeniably undergoing a process of social maturation. Businesses, universities and civic forces share in this process. This could mean a conservative consecration of the status quo, or it could mean more responsible and creative efforts to meet population change. There is also a steady educational upgrading of the urban population. This development may be the most hopeful by far, since it could lead not only to an increase of tolerance and a decline of racial superstition but to the elimination of those cultural lags in the population that undermine civic harmony. It is not the total years of average school attendance that will aid us in this matter, however, but our ability to educate in depth according to the classical and humanist ideals.

The change in urban affairs that will probably be most notable will be the accession of the non-white population to effective political power in the large cities. The estrangement between city and suburb is fated to be with us for many years because of the way in which local autonomy and independence is rooted in our government and popular social thinking. During this period the central cities will be very important in the political mosaics of state and federal affairs. The suburbs are likely to tend increasingly toward political independence and factionalism. Such conditions seem to be inherent in the sprawling suburban areas that will be evolving for decades yet. The central cities, though, are tending toward a more single-minded emphasis upon their needs and their political power in relation to rurally dominated state legislatures. The same seems to be true of their position with regard to Federal policies and programs. There is a clearer perception of the urban pressures in the central cities with their strong power elites, active communications and heavy voting strength. The increasing involvement and eventual leadership of non-whites in the large city political machines will have a great effect upon the legal and governmental attitude toward racial problems.

Leadership Lag

The leadership and "power structure" within the metropolitan areas is as complex as the urban centers themselves. There are, as has been suggested, a series of elites representing different community elements. These are the "old family" patricians, the managerial elite of commercial and industrial note, the cadre of middle-class civic leaders, the socially conscious elements of the government bureaucracies, the labor leaders and so on.[12] The position of leadership, however, imposes certain attitudes on the entire cross-section of the urban power structure. The leaders of the vast and complex metropolitan centers are still largely of white stock and have inherited the distorted racial ideas of the past. These leaders are impatient with social problems, often because of a keenly felt individualism. They have not traditionally, and do not now, welcome changes they cannot control. Racial change, like the foreign immigration of the past, is in this category, and the urban leaders look on the racial population shift with great misgivings.[13] Leadership has an alternative to confronting such problems as racial segregation in the urban core—the white suburbs offer scope for constructive activity and preoccupation. Thus the elite of the metropolitan areas, for a variety of reasons, does not view the racial change in population with confidence or equanimity.[14]

But the manpower needs of technical society will not permit any quarantine of the large non-white group. The size of the non-white population, its mobility and aspirations simply cannot be ignored, no matter what the reluctance of the urban leaders. Every institution in the metropolis is affected by the needs and advancement of the minority population. Commerce, industry, public affairs, education and residential life are all

touched by the change in the composition of the population.
The response of urban leadership has been to profess a somewhat vague brotherhood code and hope that the strain between
segregation and the movement of desegregation will not alter
leadership patterns too drastically.

The first needs of minority groups have traditionally been
met in the urban environment by governmental remedies
achieved through political pressure. The non-political leaders
have assented to this procedure not only because of commitment to the democratic ideal but because the governmental
remedies frequently represented an easy accommodation and
permitted a sort of civic stalemate. Political concessions in
terms of fair employment laws, a few judgeships, some public
housing and access to public facilities have given recognition
and some status to the minority groups. Although such politically devised benefits have been satisfactory for minorities
in the past, they are increasingly being recognized as mere
stopgaps. Full participation in an affluent democratic urban
society is an even more attractive goal. The pace and dimensions of modern social change reveal the old quasi-solutions
for the half-measures they are. It would be folly for urban
leaders to believe that the metropolitan segregation system can
be long preserved by politically enacted substitutes for genuine
equality and social acceptance for minorities.

The reliance upon politically motivated devices has prevented the urban leadership echelons from taking the initiative
on a broad scale to alter racial ideas and practices in the major cities in any adequate way. This failure of initiative has
left the racial issue at the mercy of popular superstition and
civic indifference. The non-political leaders, with few exceptions, have studiously refrained from demonstrating a positive
personal interest in dealing with racial problems. Contributions to civil rights and "brotherhood" agencies are made, but

the basic task of renovating the racial practices of the major urban institutions is largely evaded and postponed. The result has been the national misfortune of massive urban segregation.[15]

Having failed to slay the dragon of racial discrimination in the days of sparse population and rural settings, democratic leadership must now contend with the dragon's seed, grown great and angry, making their lair in the labyrinth of the metropolis. To deal with the tensions and difficulties arising out of big-city segregation, a very thoroughgoing dedication is called for. The only way in which the vast segregated areas can take advantage of the opportunity for voluntary dispersion is gradually. Their size precludes any swift diffusion, and only demagogues pretend otherwise. The dedication required of men who are concerned with this issue, therefore, is one that must stand the test of time. Short-term commitments will not help to solve an historic problem of such long duration. The sources of this required dedication will not be brotherhood luncheons, slogan campaigns, or television exhortations; it must be drawn from the deepest deposits of religion and idealism in the American experience.

But altruism and the unflagging resolution to rid the cities of racist practices will not be successful unless they are accompanied by a clear understanding of the social factors that animate and surround the institution of segregation. In a nation famed for its pragmatic approach to various problems, it is curious that the problem of segregation has been approached in such an impractical way. Reformers have tried to abolish the evil solely with the fiery rhetoric of religion. The stone barriers of segregation have been attacked with the chisels of legislation and the rams of Constitutional principle. But there has not really been a great deal of study of the problem. Only in the last twenty years have competent social scientists and historians begun to delve into the hidden sources of racism.

Segregation Studies

Perhaps it is the casual attitude of Americans toward academic study, now happily passing, that has retarded a factual and comprehensive approach toward the racial schism conserved by residential segregation. Over three decades ago some central truths about the problem were recognized, but they seem to have been all but lost in the stream of superficial commentary.

Ernest Burgess was aware in 1928 that residential segregation was the result, not of racism alone, but "of the interplay of factors in urban growth which determine the location and movement of all groups, institutions and individuals."[16] In 1930 Louise Kennedy, in *The Negro Peasant Turns Cityward*, set forth the special character of Negro residential difficulties, hinting at the psychological damage that was to be such a notable argument in the apologetics of race relations in later years.[17] Harvard historian M. L. Hanson, in 1940, affirmed that Northern segregation had not so shaken Negro confidence in the "American Dream" that Negroes had to change their view of the nation as one of a land of opportunity.[18]

In 1943, at the urging of Gunnar Myrdal, Charles S. Johnson of Fisk University published *Patterns of Negro Segregation*, a broad but nonetheless penetrating survey of segregation practices as they affected a variety of social institutions. A consideration of spatial segregation practices and restrictive laws aimed at housing gave a historical perspective on residential segregation in the South, the border states and Northern centers. Johnson, a wonderfully knowledgeable student of race relations, stated that "the racial segregation in residential areas provides the basic structure for other institutional forms of segregation." [19] Johnson's book is one of the few treatments of segregation which accord spatial separation its logical priority and position in the study of race relations. Although the analysis of housing patterns in this book is acute, the treatment is not extensive.

By 1944 Gunnar Myrdal had produced the first encyclopedic study of modern American racial problems. Wide-ranging as it was, *The American Dilemma* did not examine residential segregation exhaustively. Myrdal saw three factors accounting for residential segregation: the hostile will of the white majority; the poverty of minority families, which reduced their access to the general housing market; the "ethnic attachment" within minority groups themselves.[20] The lack of elaboration on this analysis was no doubt the result of Myrdal's necessity of synthesizing.

In 1948 Robert Weaver published *The Negro Ghetto*, the first major book-length treatment of residential housing segregation by a competent analyst. Racial restrictions in housing had been the subject of limited comment in sociological literature since the urban sociologists of the University of Chicago had pioneered in the study of slum conditions in the 1920's. Various attempts to define the problem of residential segregation had been made as far back as W. E. B. Du Bois's research into Philadelphia conditions in 1909.[21] It remained for Robert Weaver to produce a scholarly and searching description of non-white housing concentration, and he did so with a facility and a grasp of the social dimensions of the subject that made his work a monument of analysis of a social problem.[22]

Weaver had gained much knowledge from his involvement with the legal campaign of the National Association for the

Advancement of Colored People (NAACP) to overturn judicial sanction of racially restrictive covenants on property. This legal effort was dramatic and represented the first phase of a great program of "emancipation by litigation" that has written civil rights history in the last twenty years. *The Negro Ghetto* reflects Weaver's preoccupation with this legal fight. He appears to overvalue the significance of the legal victories that made restrictive covenants unenforceable in the courts with the Supreme Court decision in Shelley vs. Kramer, in 1948. Writing from the perspective of 1959, a later student of housing segregation suggests that the legal nullity of restrictive covenants has not greatly diminished the effectiveness of housing segregation forces.[23]

The next landmark in the work of measuring the Goliath of housing segregation was *Forbidden Neighbors,* by Charles Abrams, published in 1955.[24] Abrams, a man of prodigious energy and gifts, and with a rich background of experience in the housing field, produced a highly readable account of the growth of housing segregation. He traced its rise in the early years of the century and detailed its establishment following the Negro migrations to the North during World War I. Abrams showed the complicity of government with the segregation system. He outlined in vivid prose the implications of housing barriers for the burgeoning city areas with their urban renewal programs, suburban expansion and population changes. In his final chapter, Abrams looks to governmental action in a variety of forms to break the segregation pattern in housing. Because of his long governmental experience, this reliance upon public action was natural, but such a reliance underestimates the complex social causation and ramification of the residential racial problem.

By 1955 the historian C. Vann Woodward, in *The Strange Career of Jim Crow,* could say that "residential segregation in

the cities, buttressed by thousands of supporters from vested
interests beyond the reach of the laws and courts, has yielded
but little to the movement against discrimination." [25] Throughout the 1950's, however, a major research program was carried on by various public and private bodies to find out more
about the subject. Public intergroup relations agencies worked
to analyze local conditions in a number of cities. The largest
single endeavor was that of the Commission on Race and Housing of the Fund for the Republic.[26] The five volumes produced
by the Commission used the tools of market analysis and field
surveys to investigate minority housing conditions and the financial and economic factors surrounding minority housing
movements in various locations across the country. The emphasis was upon market reactions and housing conditions.

The tactics, dynamics and proximate features of residential
segregation are seldom treated at length in the studies mentioned above. It is hoped that this book will shed some addi-
tional light on these latter aspects.

Knowledge Needed

If urban leaders were to inform themselves of the problems
surrounding racial segregation through the major works dealing with the subject, the knowledge they would acquire would
be limited. The emphasis in the works is on legal review and
brief historical retrospect, descriptive summaries of housing
conditions and market analysis. The literature on the subject
now current is fragmentary and highly variable in quality.
Much of the most comprehensive and specific knowledge of
residential segregation and racial change is the intellectual
property of a small cadre of individuals who are members of

the National Association of Intergroup Relations Officials, a professional association of persons in intergroup work.[27]

What is growing with respect to the subject is an adequate theory and conceptual outline of the social process of racial concentration and movement, and a thorough social documentation of this process as it relates to residential activity. This book is an attempt to further this task by examining urban conditions. It is an attempt to enumerate the factors that govern and influence racial movement in the urban environment. Whatever the need for academic study of this subject may be, the exigencies of civic decision and urban change will not wait until all of the verifiable data is compiled. Those who are in positions of decision and men who have the will to serve the common good of their cities need at least a schematic knowledge of the forces animating racial change today. This book, based upon daily experience in dealing with racial change in an urban setting, may provide some of this knowledge.

If leaders of life in the cities can gain an understanding of the multiple factors inducing racial concentration and change, they may be able to deal with the process in a constructive manner. Such an effort would be a logical and restorative development of our democratic life. Those who contend that efforts to induce, guide, or structure racial change are authoritarian meddling or presumptuous social folly are in an utterly contradictory position. Frequently such critics are the very ones who encouraged the manipulation of social change when industrialization was being fostered. They seldom question the promotion of social change through commercialized mass media for the benefit of profit-making enterprise. That their dissent is registered when racial change is in question is indicative of a double standard.

A more serious misgiving is that which questions whether there can be compatability between democratic social patterns,

racial or otherwise, and the technology-dominated mass society.[28] There has been in our century a deep undercurrent of
doubt emanating from men who see an essential contradiction
between the democratic ethic of citizen responsibility and the
bureaucracy and technical organization of mass society. The
American tradition of urban reform has been one of simplified
crusades.[29] If we are to raise the ethical norms and work out
the democratic ideals of our society, we must do so in the midst
of all the complexities and large-scale problems of the urban
environment. This test is at the center of the moral dilemma of
modern society. It involves such problems as those of the reorganization of government and the reshaping of education to
meet the needs of our new world. It also involves the abiding
difficulties of race relations. In this latter field democracy has
many marks against it on the liabilities side of the ledger; in
education and government our successes have been much more
pronounced. The fact is that in government and education we
have available to us the best social experience of the Western
tradition, whereas the problems of our race relations are in a
sense peculiar to ourselves. There is little that we can learn
from the other Western nations about the process of racial
unification and the practical development of harmony. The
issues presented by race relations will be part of the trial of our
civic virtues and integrity in the decades immediately ahead.
These issues may well be the critical tests of our ability to
create a synthesis between democratic traditions, values and
ethics and the powerful elements of modern mass society.

NOTES

1. The Committee for Economic Development, *Guiding Metropolitan Growth* (New York, August 1960), p. 5. At the turn of the
century 90% of all Negro Americans lived in the South and more

than 75% in rural areas. By 1950 more than 62% of these were urban dwellers and one third of American Negroes lived outside the South.

2. "Never before in the history of the world have great groups of people so diverse in background been thrown together in such close contacts as in the cities of America. The typical American city, therefore, does not consist of a homogeneous body of citizens, but of human beings with the most diverse cultural backgrounds. . . ." National Resources Committee, *Our Cities: Their Role in the National Economy* (Washington, D.C., U. S. Government Printing Offices, 1937), p. 10.

3. See Samuel Lubell, *The Future of American Politics* (Garden City, New York, Doubleday, 1956), pp. 61-85, for a description of ethnic group politics.

4. See The Editors of Fortune Magazine, *The Exploding Metropolis* (Garden City, New York, 1958).

5. Robert C. Wood, *Suburbia, Its People and Their Politics* (Boston, Houghton, 1958), p. 86.

6. The study *Guiding Metropolitan Growth* calls this situation "Fractionated government."

7. Negroes are still the outstanding exception to the general urban ecological cycle of concentration and dispersion. See Stuart A. Queen and D. B. Carpenter, *The American City* (New York, McGraw, 1953), p. 107.

8. U.S. Dept. of Commerce, Bureau of Census, Series Census, A.M.S.C.P.—27 No. 29.

9. Dennis Clark, "Racism in the North," *The Commonweal,* March 1957.

10. R. M. Moss, Associate Director of the National Urban League, has stated: "Housing is the key to the employment situation in the industrial centers. Experience with anti-Negro discrimination in housing has proven that it is possible to exclude any group from housing by excluding it from employment." Quoted by Rev. John LaFarge, S.J., in *The Catholic Viewpoint on Race Relations* (Garden City, Hanover House, New York, 1960), p. 89. See Walter Reuther's remarks before the U. S. Civil Rights Commission, *New York Times,* December 15, 1960, and the 1960 Annual Report of the President's Committee on Government Contracts, *New York Times,* January 12, 1960. See also A. McLee, "The Impact of Seg-

regated Housing on Public Schools," in W. Bolckman and S. Lehrer, *The Countdown on Segregated Education* (New York, Society for Advancement of Education, 1960).

11. David Riesman, *The Lonely Crowd* (New Haven, Yale University Press, 1950).

12. C. Wright Mills, *The Power Elite* (New York, Oxford University Press, 1956), p. 36.

13. Oscar Handlin, *The Newcomers* (Cambridge, Harvard University Press, 1960), "The Historical Background."

14. Some exceptions to this may be seen in the record of support for stable, integrated residential patterns on the part of the Greater Baltimore Committee. See The Sidney Hollander Foundation, *Toward Equality* (1960), p. 46. ACTION Housing in Pittsburgh is another such example of concern.

15. Carl T. Rowan, "The Negro in the North," *Saturday Evening Post,* October 12, 1957.

16. "Residential Segregation in American Cities," *Annals of American Academy of Political and Social Science* (November 1928), p. 115.

17. New York, Columbia University Press, 1930.

18. *The Immigrant in American History* (Cambridge, Harvard University Press, 1940), Introduction.

19. New York, Harper, 1943, p. 8.

20. New York, Harper, 1944, p. 619.

21. *The Philadelphia Negro* (Philadelphia, Ginn, 1909).

22. *The Negro Ghetto* (New York, Harcourt, 1948).

23. Clement E. Vose, *Caucasians Only* (Los Angeles and Berkeley, University of California Press, 1959). "The fact that racial segregation in the residential areas of America's largest cities has not been altered to any substantial degree suggests the limited potency of court victories in some cases" (p. IX).

24. New York, Harper, 1959, p. 304.

25. New York, Oxford, 1955. "Residential segregation in the cities, buttressed by thousands of supporters from vested interests beyond the reach of laws and courts, has yielded but little to the movement against discrimination. Perhaps the most significant gain registered has been the Supreme Court decision of 1948 that held invalid the judicial enforcement of private restrictions covenants on the ground that they deprived minorities of their right to equal protection of the laws. The spread of public housing and the in-

creased participation of the federal government in the financing
and regulation of housing development have had some effect. But,
on the whole, residential separation of the races is the prevailing
principle."

26. See Davis McEntire, *Residence and Race* (Berkeley and Los Angeles, University of California Press, 1960).
27. The National Office of this group is at 2027 Massachusetts Avenue, N.W., Washington 6, D.C.
28. Walter Lippmann, *The Public Philosophy* (New York, Mentor Books, New American Library, 1956), p. 85.
29. Richard Hofstadter, *The Age of Reform* (New York, Knopf, 1955).

2

Segregation's Sequence

IN ORDER to understand the development and prevalence of residential segregation, it is necessary to have some knowledge of the physical circumstances that have been associated with its growth. The man-made geography of the great cities has been the background for the growth of large-scale housing segregation. The slums and tenements, the high-rise apartment areas, row-house neighborhoods and middle-class subdivisions have all served as settings for racial change. The various kinds of housing and neighborhoods have been extremely important in determining the manner in which racial change has occurred and the ways in which segregation has been consolidated. The factors of housing quality, density of dwellings on the land and neighborhood composition have established the physical context in which the dynamics of racial separation have worked. The physical features of the urban landscape have themselves been in a process of change that has interacted with the shift of population and housing demand. Surprisingly little has been written about the influence of city landmarks and topography upon the shape of segregation.

The Limiting Landscape

The physical circumstances surrounding minority groups determine many things about their movement. They determine the economics that will be involved in the movement or segregation of the group. The class level at which the racial problem is enacted is usually matched by the physical usages in the area. The kind of housing structures in question have a great deal to do with the rate at which racial change or division takes place. Neighborhood layout and residential construction also do much to predetermine the basic psychology that will prevail in relation to racial matters in a given area. Thus the physical environment can be very revealing to inquirers who seek to analyze trends in minority population movement.

Physical landmarks and divisions are significant in most cases because of the psychological function they perform. They permit ethnic groups to establish barriers and boundaries corresponding to their desires for social separation. These factors enable racial opinion to erect clearly discernible boundaries between respective groups. In densely populated and highly mobile urban areas this becomes very important to people. Home purchases, business locations, school boundaries and service areas have often been charted in relation to physical boundaries that represent lines of racial demarcation. Occasionally the physical features do represent natural barriers to community development of any kind. Physical boundaries, whether they are simple natural obstacles to movement or socially contrived barriers designated by custom, are something of a guarantee of the racial status quo.

A few illustrations will indicate the concrete ways in which physical features affect the distribution of non-whites in urban areas. An analysis of the racial distribution maps of major

cities and some knowledge of racial movement in these centers bring such situations to light.[1] Natural topographical factors have been obstacles to racial movement in some places. The Harlem River divided the huge Negro population of Harlem from the white residential areas of the Bronx for years. The Cuyahoga River in Cleveland cut the city into two segments, one accessible to Negroes and one largely all-white. The fashionable slopes of the mountains that thread through Los Angeles were known humorously to Negroes for a time as "the white highlands," a phrase suggestive of the white man's preserves in Kenya. The predilection of upper-class groups for high ground was influential in such an instance, of course.

Frequently a combination of streets, railroads or land uses is combined in local segregation tradition to define the limits of a racial ghetto. In San Francisco the westernmost non-white "compound" was clearly bounded in the 1940's by Arguello Boulevard on the North, Geary Street on the East and State Street on the South. The eastern area of Negro concentration was marked by a triangle formed roughly by Market Street on the South and Columbus Avenue and Pacific Avenue on the North.[2]

In Chicago the northern tier of the Negro community was marked in the period following World War II by the Chicago and Northwestern Railway above Lake Street in Central Chicago. In South Chicago the Union Stock Yards and the long line of Stewart Avenue and the New York Central Line have been the limits of westward Negro expansion. The Stewart Avenue Line is a boundary marking the opposition of the foreign-language neighborhoods to expansion of the Negro population. A similar boundary line set up along an arterial traffic street could be seen in Detroit in the early 1940's, where Woodward Avenue marked off Negro and white residential districts. In Newark, New Jersey, two railroad lines and an interchange

of the Jersey Turnpike set off a Negro from a white area in a
locale with the interesting designation of "Ironbound."[3]

When racial change does occur, the segregation process re-
defines the boundaries of non-white expansion by seeking out
new landmarks. The change may occur first adjacent to the
original boundary, particularly if the bounding element is a
blighting element, such as an offensive railroad trackage or
industrial land use. Or the racial change may use a bounding
arterial street as the channel for movement. In Detroit, Oak-
man Boulevard was extended like a "protecting arm" part of
the way around the Russell Woods area.[4] The Boulevard was
the racial boundary beyond which Negroes did not move until
about 1955. Then racial change moved along this perimeter
and eventually into the neighborhood proper. Racial change
in Philadelphia's western edge followed a similar course along
Cobbs Creek Parkway. Elsewhere in Philadelphia the movement of Negroes in the 1940's and 1950's extended to several
definite lines and then stopped. Lehigh Avenue in North Philadelphia was one of these lines; another was formed by the
Reading Railroad commuter tracks that form an arc north of
Germantown beyond which Negroes have not moved.[5]

As population shifts according to housing demand, or as
urban redevelopment alters physical landmarks and sites, the
process of psychological demarcation and the setting of racial
boundaries by custom continues. This has become a very active
process since World War II. The new mobility of minority families in the large cities and the great housing turnover induced
by the pull of suburbia have brought great changes. Old barriers have been jumped or circumvented. New ones have arisen,
but they will be harder to maintain, because even a minimal
dispersion of the minority tends to overcome them. The pos-
sibilities of such dispersion are increasing greatly. It may be
that in the future the landmarks and boundaries that denote

racial partition will become significant more in terms of social class than of racial segregation.

The mobility of the population in large urban centers is well known. This mobility is one of the characteristics of our cities.[6] The mobility within the old city neighborhoods to which Negroes have been confined has stemmed from various causes in recent years. In-migration has been a major factor. Goldstein's studies of mobility of this type show the high rate of non-white influx in a typical urban satellite city.[7] The 1950 census was a revelation in this respect also.[8] Economic privation that drives families from one unit to another in search of cheaper rents or better heating is a strong influence. Many minority families, hit by the economic recessions of the 50's, or having become part of a glut of unskilled labor in a market increasingly geared to higher job skills, had to change dwellings because they fell behind in one or two rent payments. Disorganized family life also promotes exchange of dwellings, and there is a tragic amount of this in the depressed city areas. Urban renewal and redevelopment projects have displaced minority families from sites in all the large cities. The greatest single motivating force behind the movement of minority families in the urban centers, however, has been the desire to overcome the housing problems that have been a traditional part of ghetto living. The desire for family improvement has been the positive element of this drive and has led to strenuous efforts to escape the old areas for newer ones.

Neighborhood Differences

The movement of minority groups in relation to physical boundaries and demarcation lines is also conditioned by housing quality and the real estate market.[9] The traditional limita-

tions upon Negro buying power have meant a high proportion
of renters among Negro families. It has also meant that areas
of obsolescent dwellings, exploited properties and dwellings
next to undesirable land uses have been consigned or have
gravitated to Negro occupancy. These facts have been the
chief determinants of Negro residential distribution. An excellent statement of this phenomenon has been made by the Commission on Race and Housing.[10] Minority families have had to
be satisfied with the leftovers of the real estate market. It might
even be argued that, by absorbing the refuse of the residential
market, the minority population has been the salvation of the
market in major cities with their vast areas of outmoded and
unimproved dwellings.

The legal framework in which the transfer of property between racial groups has been effected has been very important.
The significance of the 1948 Supreme Court decision in Shelley
vs. Kramer should be noted here. This decision, as was stated
in Chapter 1, made racial restrictions on property unenforceable in the courts. Had restrictive covenants been legally in
force in the 1940's and 1950's, the movement of non-whites
would have had to advance through an unending quagmire
of litigation. Rent control laws, poor housing code enforcement and legal but nefarious land contracts and lease purchase
contracts have put legal pitfalls enough in the path of minority
families acquiring property. Great damage has been done when
minority families, foregoing legal counsel, have fallen prey to
the vicious and exploitive practices applied wholesale to unsus-
pecting home buyers and hard-pressed slum families.[11]

The rate at which property is utilized has been a strong influence in directing the course and the sequence of racial movement. The number of dwellings on the land in a given neighborhood affects not only the outlook and the conditions of
racial change but the pace at which Negroes become part of

the locality. Neighborhoods which are built up at high densities are usually dominated by rental apartment units. Residents of such areas seldom have a deep or organized concern for neighborhood matters. An impersonal attitude prevails. The properties are owned by absentee investors and managed by business corporations unconcerned with the social problems of the area except as they affect financial returns and investment future. In such high-density areas, racial change is not usually a matter that affects the personal financial resources of the residents, and its emotional impact is diminished by the general impersonality of the residential situation. The residents may resent the change according to stereotyped views; they may complain of what they feel to be an affront and an inconvenience, but they are not so firmly wedded to the area as home owners would be. They are relatively free to leave a situation that they deem undesirable and a threat to their social status. As a result, the movement of whites out of such an area tends to be precipitous. Some areas in New York have undergone racial change rather slowly despite densities of more than two hundred families per acre. This is because the housing shortage in New York during the 1940's and 1950's prevented ready movement. In Chicago, however, where racial attitudes seem to be more antagonistic, there have been some classic "panic" turnovers of population in apartment areas.[12]

In low-density areas with high rates of home ownership the sense of attachment to the locality has often been built up over the years. There is more reluctance to leave, and the financial and legal problems involved in the sale of homes retard the rapid exodus of the residents.[13] Even in these circumstances, however, it is not unusual for a block of houses to change racial occupancy completely in the course of two years. Most of the material written about racial change in housing is focused upon such areas. There is much less homogeneity in such neighborhoods than is supposed, however. They are frequently spotted with rental dwellings, illegal apartments and other property uses that complicate transition.

In older districts where non-residential land uses are encroaching or already scattered about, where the structures no longer meet popular housing tastes or have simply deteriorated in value, racial change can be a swift and utterly disruptive phenomenon. Areas that are dilapidated or going downhill toward slum conditions represent a wide variety of property holdings and treatment. Most slums are not predominantly the holdings of huge, soulless corporations. The properties are usually owned by "little people," who have inherited them or have made some modest investments in them.[14] The greed that exploits the slums is the cumulative greed and neglect of thousands of little property-owners, most of them absentees.[15] Their exploitation of people and property is aided by a corps of professional brokers, agents and managers. These are more often the true "slumlords," for they frequently have large investments in the depressed areas as well as the management of a number of dilapidated rental units. These slum operators are small fish in the vast ocean of urban economics, but like many small fish they are voracious and alert. They are, of course, related to the large and respectable banks and mortgage companies, which will receive their business without scruple or question.

The deteriorated areas, which should be more appropriately known as "exploitation" areas, are today largely Negro-occupied. Although the 1960 census reveals a considerable increase in home ownership among non-whites and some gains with regard to overcrowding and the occupancy of substandard dwellings, there are still huge numbers crammed into the exploitation areas. In these districts, the climax areas for family breakdown, personality disorder and all the worst urban social problems, the minority families become the victims of discrimination and speculation in a wicked cycle. Their occupancy of such areas is used as an argument to reinforce segregation so that their residence in slum conditions will be perpetuated. The profligate use of property in these districts is blamed upon the Negro occupants. The fact is that these occupants are usually only the instruments or the proximate cause of property abuse. The real causes are the absenteeism, the wantonly intensive use of structures, the corrupt housing-code enforcement and the personal greed that produce the slum.

Racial change in areas where property is extensively abused and has deteriorated can be a fearsome thing. The low educational level of the occupants whose misfortunes force them into slums and semi-slums increases the possibility that violence may erupt. The change takes place under exploitive conditions. Families of both races with limited ability to move freely are made to pay dearly for entrance to and exit from the slum. Juvenile gangs may contest the change literally on a foot-by-foot basis, waging warfare in the streets. In some areas, though, a camaraderie of the afflicted does grow up, and whites and Negroes of low social status fraternize and make common cause in their struggle for subsistence.[16] Thus, while the common ties of humanity remain undiscovered in psychiatric clinics and college-bred suburban salons, the trials of slum life sometimes suddenly bring them to light.

The foregoing paragraphs illustrate the way in which the abuse of property and the conversion of land to a different use in residential environments affect the development and rate of racial change.

How Change Begins

How does racial change begin in city neighborhoods? If segregation lines and restrictive practices are zealously maintained, what events initiate the flow of minority families from
one area into another? The answers to these questions are complex. They are part of the devious complexity of the modern
city itself. Here are some of the ways in which racial change
has begun:

1.   Properties in an area may become obsolete in structure or state of repair or too old to be desirable among white
home buyers who have various alternative locations open to
them. Minority buyers will then be funneled into such a neighborhood simply because they represent the only available economic demand.

2.   Properties may lose their appeal for white occupants,
who can move elsewhere, owing to the encroachment of some
offensive land use. A slaughterhouse, a wool-processing plant
or a freight terminal moving into an older neighborhood may
divert white demand from the area and induce eventual Negro
occupancy.[17]

3.   Some vocational group may abandon an area to seek
employment in another locale. If minority families are adjacent, this may be the occasion for them to replace the original
group. The impact of Prohibition, for instance, upon several
big-city neighborhoods where German brewery workers lived
caused these families to move from blocks near closed brew-
eries. Negroes replaced them. Hastily built wartime housing
units, abandoned by whites with the diminution of labor demand in adjacent industries, have been occupied by Negro
families.

4. Real estates speculators have triggered racial change by inserting a Negro family, preferably a disreputable one, into an area and then exploiting the fear and distress of white families to promote property turnover. In Chicago this process resulted in quick and handsome profits for speculators. Selling a house to Negroes for twice the price of its purchase from whites was not uncommon.[18]

5. Minority housing demand has at times been so urgent that it simply overwhelmed an area. Purchases have been made at inflated prices from individual owners whose desire for profit has overcome their racial antagonism. In such cases the first purchases are often made independently of the real estate broker fraternity, who then usually abandon their role as guardians of the racial homogeneity of the area to join in the wholesale exchanges.

6. Public housing, which in many communities is integrated or heavily non-white in occupancy, may bring about change in a neighborhood. Negro families emerging from the project may rent or purchase nearby. Whites, feeling threatened by the presence of a low-rent project, may yield their houses to nearby Negro families.

7. Physical barriers that served as lines of racial demarcation may be moved by business decisions or urban redevelopment. The replacement of old traffic arteries by new expressway routes sometimes decreases the significance of these streets as boundaries. Redevelopment can also promote racial change by displacing Negro families and relocating them in all-white areas.

8. Sometimes resistance to racial change on the part of civic groups crumbles, and Negroes gain entry through normal purchasing channels. Actually there have been very few effective, long-term organized groups in Northern cities dedicated to excluding Negroes. This is because there have been few

effective, long-term organized local neighborhood groups of any kind in urban areas. Defending segregation has largely been the work of the housing industry itself.

9. Houses sold at public auction to the highest bidder may be purchased by Negroes. Dwellings repossessed by the Federal Housing Administration (FHA) and the Veterans Administration (VA) because of mortgage default must, according to Federal directive, be sold without discrimination as to race, religion or national origin. However, such resales are usually handled through local real estate brokers, who frustrate the non-discrimination procedure.

10. Negroes with sufficient income to circumvent racially restrictive pressures may purchase homes in "exclusive" or "fashionable" areas. Such persons may be of such stature and economic ability that they can defy local taboos.

11. Negroes with sufficient income may actually precede white occupants in a developing area and maintain their homes as whites gradually surround them. Their presence may later bring other Negroes to the area.

12. A neighbor may sell an isolated property to a Negro out of spite, as a form of revenge or retaliation against another neighbor who has been an antagonist in a local dispute. Persons who have tried to obtain a zoning variance and been successfully opposed by their neighbors, for instance, sometimes feel they can retaliate by "selling to colored."

13. A minority family may buy a property through a "straw man," through an intermediary or under a fictitious business name, and surprise an all-white community by occupying the secretly acquired house. There are some legal pitfalls inherent in this procedure, particularly if government mortgage insurance is sought, but the practice of "straw buying" is common enough, although its use to effect racial change has been rather limited.

14.   A minority family may rent or buy a home by availing itself of the provisions of a fair housing practices law. Such
laws, if patiently utilized, can gain houses for families despite
discrimination. For example, two Negro families won a suit
against William Levitt over entry into Levittown, New Jersey.

15.   Some families may enter an all-white area through the
programs of such groups as Friends Suburban Housing and
the Greater Minneapolis Fair Housing Program. These groups
bring together a willing white seller, usually a person of al-
truistic convictions, and a qualified minority buyer. The activities of such groups do not account for a great number of such
placements, but they represent practical business approaches
toward overcoming total segregation in housing.

This list does not exhaust the ways in which racial change
can begin in city neighborhoods, but it indicates the diversity
of conditions which may be involved.

Cycles of Change

Since 1940 the passage of the minority population over
physical boundaries and customary limits has become a game
of geographic leapfrog. This transfer of people has been set
against a background of continued competition for land in urban areas and the active exchange of property induced by a period of prosperity. As cycles of change have swept across the
urban landscape, bringing racial change with them, social
scientists have devised terms to describe the process of population movement. If we utilize these terms, we can gain further
insight into the dynamics of racial movement.[19]

Access denotes the process whereby a group gains entry to
an area. The increased earning powers of Negroes due to wartime and post-war employment opportunities and the pressing

housing needs developed during a time of housing shortage induced Negro families to venture beyond the confines of the pre-war ghettos. The location of wartime emergency housing projects and the settlement of non-white labor near new industrial developments placed Negroes within bidding range of previously all-white dwelling areas.

Competition describes the attempts of groups to dominate an area, either economically or culturally. The competition may not be conscious, but it will include the physical presence of a group in a given area. In Detroit and in Chicago where wartime industry had swollen minority populations, there was intense competition for housing. One Chicago tenement manager succeeded briefly in operating swing-shift rental units on the basis of a daytime clientele for whites and a Negro clientele at night. The competition for an area means competition for its institutions as well. Indeed the purchase of a church, an apartment house or restaurant by a minority group may set in motion the entire process of competition for an area.

Succession denotes the actual replacement of one group by another. This has not been uncommon in urban neighborhoods with histories of seriatim occupancy by different ethnic elements. The replacement of one group by another may reveal a definite connection between the groups. Popular opinion about ethnic matters may link certain minority groups together, thereby providing an expectancy and the conditions for the replacement of one particular group by another. In some cities those of Asian origin are considered to be the forerunners of the Negro group in residential movement.[20] Jews, Puerto Ricans, Portuguese, American Indians—any group currently identified with minority status—may by its entry or presence induce succession by another minority group.

Equilibrium is a condition of population balance in which respective groups utilize facilities fully and offset one another's presence and needs. The groups may be rigidly segregated from one another or distributed according to a vague borderline. The scientific concept of equilibrium relates more to a balance between population and resources than it does to a balance between groups. The term is helpful, however, since it is more precise than "integrated." The term "integrated area" implies a fusion of elements, whereas an area in "equilibrium" connotes a balanced relationship between elements. Areas in a state of racial equilibrium are not easy to find. The process of segregation has worked relentlessly to destroy equilibrium and steadily consecrate neighborhoods to the occupancy of one racial group or the other.[21]

The sociologist Ernest Burgess analyzed racial change according to a set of classifications similar to those above.[22] His terms of invasion, reaction, influx and climax offer an alternative description. A consideration of racial change from the point of view of the degree of minority group representation in an area suggests descriptives that indicate the proportionate numbers of the group in a neighborhood i.e., "pioneer" representation, light, heavy, maximum. Both these classifications permit the designation of segregation as a terminal status.

Patterns on the Maps

The pattern by which racial change proceeds in residential areas is important in providing the conditions for the full enactment of the segregation process. Racial change may proceed along major arteries surrounding and defining an area, for instance, and then "fill in" the area so described, following the canons of segregated market activity. This kind of racial change moving around the circumference of a neighborhood may occur through the rental of apartments above blocks of small businesses and stores along heavy-traffic streets. Having occupied these units, Negro families may then filter back into the neighborhood proper behind the business blocks.

At times racial change may be begun by the movement of a single institution into an area. A Negro church that manages to relocate in a white area may gradually attract its adherents into a locality. Such an island of minority residents may later spread or be linked to other such areas to become belts of segregation. In some cities there have been little communities of Negroes who served as domestics and handymen in middle-class or upper-class neighborhoods. Usually these families would occupy a few back streets in the area or be allotted a cluster of rundown dwellings next to a railroad track. In times of high vacancy rates or general housing change, these fragments of non-white occupancy can become the basis for the expansion of minority residence throughout the entire community. If a once desirable middle-class area becomes less favored because of the attraction of suburbia for whites, the resulting "softness" in the local market can expand initial pockets of Negro residence into general patterns of minority occupancy.

There is evidence that minority group families may follow lines of transportation in extending their patterns of occupancy. Puerto Rican families certainly seem to have done this in New York City. Cheap subway transit which was convenient to the service areas of the city that employed unskilled labor created clusters of Puerto Ricans adjacent to subway stops.[23] This kind of movement fits into the "sector theory" of linear urban movement and development proposed by the noted land economist Homer Hoyt. There do not seem to be carefully verified examples of such movement for Negroes.

On occasion there are opportunities for "colonization" of small areas in all-white outlying sections of the cities. Some builders may develop a small group of homes especially for Negroes, or perhaps for integrated occupancy. This kind of "jumping" movement is quite infrequent. It usually results in small "colonies" of Negroes, surrounded by white residents who do their best to ignore the minority grouping.

Another way by which patterns of minority residence change is through what could be termed dispersal. In some city areas it is possible for some single minority families to venture into all-white areas and to obtain and maintain homes in such areas. This kind of movement takes place under considerable strain and tension in most cases, it is true. It is not significant for its numerical alteration of segregation patterns, but it does represent the beginning of integration where one or a few Negro families are able to live on a desegregated basis in predominantly white communities without inducing extensive racial turnover and panic. Although this kind of movement has not been typical of minority residential change thus far, the fact that it can be accomplished is extremely significant for the future.

By far the most common pattern of expansion of Negro residence is a gradual "frontal" movement taking place at the edges of areas that are already large-scale segregated districts. This kind of expansion of minority residence may begin on a small scale, but the pressure of minority population behind it soon rolls it steadily along until it has reached a new barrier or developed a new racial equilibrium for the particular section of the city in which it occurs. This extension of segregation at the edges of the ghetto typifies the kind of change experienced since World War II. It is massive and steady. It adds to the deep segregation rings that surround the core of the city. It is the kind of racial movement which, in the last thirty years, has turned segregation from a negligible city phenomenon into a vast urban institution. The withdrawal of the white population before the frontal advance of the colored, and the conditions under which it has taken place, have had the most profound effects upon racial attitudes. Racial movement in this form is an overwhelming occurrence, and frequently it takes place according to the most exploitive code of real estate exchange. Even in a society with racial traditions and attitudes much more liberal than those prevailing in this country, a movement of racial groups which constituted a sort of population avalanche would disrupt social and racial harmony.

The existence of huge "glaciers" of racial segregation built up by extensions of the latter type has created great problems for urban government. The exodus of relatively well-to-do white populations from old neighborhoods has concentrated underprivileged Negro populations in the dilapidated central city areas. This has imposed a severe strain on the budgets and services of urban governments. This problem is one of the major issues of urban administration today.[24]

Expansion Areas

There are certain conditions that must exist before substantial racial change can come about. We could even say that in view of past experience in cities of the North and West, large-scale racial movement cannot take place without these conditions being present together at one time. Areas where practically all racial change takes place under the segregation system could be designated as "expansion areas." In these areas the pre-conditions for expansion would prevail. The exception to this would be neighborhoods to which only one or a few Negroes could gain access. The conditions that would mark a neighborhood as an "expansion area" for racial change within the framework of the residential segregation system are:

a.   Vacancies in dwellings and opportunity for movement into housing. Such a condition could come into being, for instance, through a high vacancy rate in existing units or through the availability of a group of new houses in an area that could not be sold to white buyers.

b.   Demand on the part of the minority families. This would require that such families be economically able to acquire houses and also that the buyers have the motivation to purchase despite the difficulties that they might encounter.

c.   Financing, for mortgages and notes must be available so that transactions can take place. Besides the equity or down-payment funds of the minority buyer, there must be a willingness on the part of the financial institutions to make mortgage money available and to deal normally with owners of rental accommodations during the period of racial change.

d.   Protection and Minimal Acceptance; for racial movement to occur in an area there must be some assurance that local opinion is moderate enough to forego extreme retaliation or campaigns to expel the minority entrants. In addition, local law enforcement authorities must assure some reasonable degree of protection to buyers faced with hostility.

Unless all above conditions are present, it is extremely unlikely that a neighborhood will become an "expansion area." Residential segregation has moved across the maps of our urban areas according to the presence of these combined factors. Intergroup relations agencies and city authorities have not become astute enough to predict the course of racial expansion. The real estate and housing industry interests which oversee the segregation system are quite irresponsible so far as the question of which areas shall become segregated next is concerned. Real estate activity is so competitive and opportunistic that a single broker can create a trend in an area where the conditions of minority demand and vacancies coincide. The white residents can even be thrown into panic to facilitate change. The financial institutions may wait until the trend is clear before endorsing the change by making their funds available on regular terms. The development of the conditions for minority expansion can be the product of conscious planning on the part of real estate men, or the conditions can be part of those apparently haphazard developments which set in motion far-reaching changes in the life of our cities.

Racial Proportions

As has been stated, most racial change in the last twenty years has taken place under conditions inducing almost total racial turnover of population in a given area. The segregation process has a strong tendency to run its course. While it is doing so, there are varying degrees of minority succession that produce differing states of neighborhood relations.

The initial phase of racial change is characterized by the presence of a small number of "pioneer" Negro families in an area. This may cause panic among residents or merely concern. The residents worry about property values and the extent that racial change may eventually reach. But at this stage there is usually little change in the institutions in the area. The churches and synagogues, the businesses and fraternal groups remain in the area.

As the residential occupancy becomes genuinely mixed in the majority of blocks, panic subsides, but the steady withdrawal of whites continues. The first businesses, the more sensitive service centers and institutions begin to leave. Barber shops and beauty salons, for instance, tend to change ownership from one race to another or to move away soon. Bars where dancing is permitted do the same. Churches or clubs whose members are resistant to accepting Negroes are likely to move. In short, those local institutions with the greatest degree of exposure to the change will move, become inactive or sell or lease their facilities to members of the new group.

When the minority group population becomes dominant in an area in actual numbers, institutions with special connections with the group become prominent and assume local leadership. Negro Baptist or Methodist churches, lodges of the Elks, NAACP branches and informal sororities and benevolent groups grow into the life of the neighborhood. As a matter of fact, businesses tend to remain owned and operated by whites for a long time, or they may continue indefinitely under absentee white ownership.

The point at which the population balance between the racial groups begins to favor the newcomers has been the subject of considerable discussion. For those working to produce stable integrated neighborhoods, the discovery of some ratio, or formula, of racial balance was felt to be important. The idea of a "tip point" has been advanced by market analyst Chester Rapkin, who believes that a stage capable of being represented as a percentage point is reached at which whites decide that they will not purchase homes in a racially mixed area. This "tip point" cannot be precisely fixed, but it seems to be defined by all commentators as one-third minority occupancy or less, with most setting it at less.

The "tip point" is more than a statistical ratio. It is a symbolic ratio of influence between two groups. It represents a juncture of social psychology and a turning point in civic opinion. The term, specifying as it does a "point," is, of course, misleading. However, experience with racial change does indicate that the flow of non-whites into an area becomes more steady and decisive after a percentage of non-white population ranging from about one third to one half has been reached.

This may be related to the fact that the opinion of white resident groups and of white prospective residents as to the thoroughness of the segregation process may now become conclusive. Another factor is the attitude of white financial institutions and real estate operators, when the decision is made to
acquiesce fully in the racial turnover.

When the segregation process does run its full course, there
is usually only residual or token occupancy of the area by
whites. Elderly people who are estranged from life in general
may be oblivious of the population shift. People who lead isolated lives, who work at night or whose jobs require much
traveling, may ignore the change. Cosmopolitans, or persons
who feel that some special mission weds them to an area, may
remain as whites who "survive" the segregation process. The
most common reason for the white populations which persist
after racial transition is the economic one. Families or individuals who would find it an economic disadvantage to move
often suppress their racial resentment and live among Negro
neighbors. Thus even in heavily segregated areas there will be
a residual white population.[25]

The sequence of segregation in the urban areas has been an
amazing thing. The practical operation of influences control-
ling minority population movement is impressive. These influences have stalled the powerful workings of urban society
where Negroes were involved. The centrifugal forces in urban
life have been thwarted by a combination of economics and
social psychology. The democratic ethic of a generally egalitarian and cosmopolitan social system has been contradicted
by our native racism. A system of racial containment has been
fixed on the mobile urban development that has characterized
the twentieth century. The retarded movement of the Negro
population in the cities has resulted in the elaboration of vast
racial concentrations at their centers which now threaten them

with service and welfare demands that are undermining their solvency.

The persistence of residential segregation based on race has also extended into the perilous atomic era a kaleidoscope of ethnic division characteristic of the century from 1850 to 1950. In permitting this, we have obstructed the mobility that is a concomitant of the urban technology we have so energetically built up. The system of sophisticated residential partition exposes a cleavage in the most prominent portion of our society which lends itself to political exploitation by our international foes in a time when our cities play hosts to thousands of keen-minded delegations from colored countries.

The physical landscapes of our cities are changing. High-speed expressway networks are linking central areas to outlying and suburban sections. Changes in the technology of home-building may make the renovation and redistribution of our urban housing supply an attainable goal in coming decades. The improvement of mass transportation is freeing labor from the necessity of residing next to industrial plant. Urban renewal is already changing wide areas of center city real estate. The areas most like to undergo physical renewal are largely occupied by non-white populations.

Physical alterations in the urban environment will be matched in coming years by new forces in the real estate market. By the late 1960's the "war babies" born in the late 1940's will be forming new families, representing an immense increase in housing turnover and demand for new houses.

The Negro population of the cities, as their buying power increases, will be constantly upgrading their housing demand. Fair housing practices laws and a growing maturity on the part of city-dwellers will begin to offset the attachment of social status to patterns of racially exclusive housing.

So deep-rooted and long-standing is the system of racial restrictions, however, that there remains some doubt whether all these influences will suffice to overcome the traditions that have artificially checked and channeled racial movements. The problem now is whether the liberating influences of economics, ethics and physical change can act as a solvent upon segregated areas so vast as to encompass hundreds of thousands of people and represent powerful racial social systems in themselves. All the new forces for change in the urban areas may result only in a more attenuated and streamlined form of segregation.

NOTES

1. The maps in Davis McEntire's *Residence and Race* give some indication of the role of streets and landmarks.
2. See maps in Volume I of *Newark—City in Transition*, prepared for the Mayor's Commission on Group Relations, Newark, New Jersey, January 1959.
3. Arthur Hoppe, "How the Fillmore Ghetto Grew," *San Francisco Chronicle*, January 13, 1959.
4. See Nathan Glazer and Davis McEntire, eds., *Studies in Housing and Minority Groups* (Berkeley and Los Angeles, University of California Press, 1960), pp. 202-203.
5. See Philadelphia Commission on Human Relations, *Non-White Residential Patterns* (June 1959).
6. Nils Anderson, *Urban Community: A World Perspective* (New York, Holt, 1959), p. 114.
7. Sidney Goldstein, *Patterns of Mobility, 1910-1950* (Philadelphia, University of Pennsylvania Press, 1958), pp. 132-133.
8. McEntire, *Residence and Race*, p. 22.
9. E. M. and R. M. Fisher, *Urban Real Estate* (New York, Holt, 1954).
10. McEntire, *Residence and Race*, ch. 7.
11. Mark J. Satter, "Land Contract Sales in Chicago," *Chicago Bar Record*, March 1958.

12. The Kenwood-Oakland area, for instance, changed with remarkable swiftness between 1943 and 1947. The Chatham area and Northwest Hyde Park also changed rapidly.

13. John McDermott, *Eight Observations about Changing Neighborhoods* (Philadelphia Commission on Human Relations, 1957).

14. Leo Grebler, *Experience in Urban Real Estate Investment* (New York, Columbia University Press, 1955), p. 183.

15. Philadelphia Housing Authority, *Relocation Report on the Norris Site* (1952).

16. See the accounts of slum fellowship in M. A. Millspaugh and G. Breckenfeld, *The Human Side of Urban Renewal* (Baltimore, Fight Blight, Inc., 1959).

17. S. L. McMichael, *McMichael's Appraising Manual* (New York, Prentice-Hall, 1947), p. 46.

18. Warren Lehman of the Chicago Commission on Human Relations in his speech, "Number of Negroes," delivered before the City Club Forum, June 23, 1959.

19. Amos Hawley, *Human Ecology* (New York, Ronald Press, 1950).

20. See U. S. Civil Rights Commission Hearings, 1960, in San Francisco and Los Angeles.

21. For stages of racial relations see E. Bogardus, "Stages of Negro-White Relations," *Sociology and Social Research*, Vol. 45, No. 1.

22. Charles S. Johnson, *Patterns of Negro Segregation* (New York, Harper, 1943), pp. 11-12.

23. H. Meyer and C. Kohn, *Readings in Urban Geography* (Chicago, Chicago University Press, 1959); see Robert T. Novack's "Distribution of Puerto Ricans in Manhattan."

24. Morton Grodzins, *The Metropolitan Area as a Racial Problem* (Pittsburgh, University of Pittsburgh Press, 1960).

25. For a listing of the type of white persons who stay in racially mixed areas see St. Clair Drake and Horace Cayton, *The Black Metropolis* (New York, Harcourt, 1955), p. 183. This list should be extended today, after the post-war experience in integration.

3

Negroes Are . . .

EVEN IN THIS MODERN AGE of mobility and impersonality, the opinion of a man's neighbors is a powerful thing. It is in the face-to-face context of the residential neighborhood that men tend to reveal themselves as they are when a pressing issue arises. On such occasions the folk mind—if we can use such a term for the urbanite's complicated beliefs—speaks for itself. The slogans and formal pronouncements of the government, the university and the pulpit are set aside, and the mind of the people expresses itself. In a complex urban society, where stereotypes and contradictions abound, there is a restraint in the larger spheres of community expression—blocs of opinion must be balanced and embarrassment must be avoided. But in the local community the restraints are less formal, and with the advent of some threat or emergency, real or imagined, the ordinary reserve and caution break down, and the man himself speaks with the full conviction of his own personal views—right or wrong.

In a nation with a proud commitment to democratic ideals and a tradition of fervent public profession of these ideals, it is not extraordinary that attitudes conflicting with these formal ideals should be maintained in an unspoken fashion below the

level of normal discourse. Every people has some such fund
of secret or unacknowledged sentiments. When these feelings
are hostile in a society that is largely genial and tolerant, there
is even more reason for reserve. So it is with racial hostility
today. In a time when the general media of communications
have been purged of the more blatant expressions of group
hostility, these expressions and their entire lexicon and rationale have entered the intellectual underground, the guarded
recesses of local community belief.

In urban society the citizen has seen great changes. The
old ethnic group life has been fading away. The expansive
freedom of individualistic American life has been increasingly
delimited by organization and controls, class ideas and elaborate codes of propriety. Many situations long abhorred have
been brought closer and closer. The citizen is now confronted
with increasing government direction and influence, a social
life of growing complexity which imposes a demand for tolerance of conflicting values—and the mingling of racial groups.
About many of these changes he can do nothing. About racial
change in many areas of life he can do nothing. But in the
residential sphere there is still a prevailing consensus against
racial integration, and there are still institutions responsive to
the pressure to forestall such change. And because this is one
change over which many people believe it is imperative to
have some control, it frequently becomes the subject of the
most intense preoccupation. It is understandable, therefore,
that the opinion of urban dwellers at the local level is something of a crisis area in the psychology of race relations and in
the resolution of a great social change.[1]

Roots of Opinion

American public opinion concerning minority residence has deep roots. It is intertwined with several centuries of intergroup history and social experience and colored by the distinctive American pattern of racial thinking. Only in a society where slavery has left such a tragic legacy and where the immigration of diverse peoples has been such a vivid national drama could our peculiar attitudes have developed. Only in a society rich enough for housing to become a status device could racial restrictions become so much of a force. Robert Weaver attributes housing segregation to a threefold source: prejudice, the influence of upper-class patterns of residential exclusion, and the fear that minorities will subvert local residential standards.[2] If we look behind this statement of causes, we can begin to see the depth from which these restrictive influences arise.

Although prejudice is sometimes a judgment without reference to the facts, it is more often a judgment without consideration of *all* the facts. There are usually some external facts or some superficial appearances evident even to the most limited mind. In the case of racial attitudes, there have been historic circumstances which provided the rude or distorted premises for prejudicial thinking. Primary among these sets of conditions was the institution of slavery.

Since slaves were regarded as a convenience as well as a necessity by those who lived by their exploitation, it was customary in the slave-holding areas for them to reside close to the dwellings of their masters.[3] True, these were the better-instructed slaves, the household slaves, but the pattern of biracial residence grew as the convenience of domestic life became steadily more dependent upon slave ministration, spreading from the rural areas to the cities of the Southern states, where town houses were supplemented by nearby quarters for slaves who were artisans or household servants.

Despite the social distance preserved, the contact between slave and master had a reality. Slaves were close enough to be known as individuals, and the circumstances of their lives were taken, however callously, into account. With the passing of slavery, the relationship altered. The fundamental fact of interdependence between the Negro and the white man became less obvious. Gradually the Negro became less of a reality and more of a creature of fantasy. This seems particularly evident in the attitudes which have given rise to the complicated system of enforced segregation. As slavery passed, the traits of slaves became, not accepted facts of a slave status, but personal attributes with a weight of reproach attached to them. If Negroes were observed to be immoral, lazy, intellectually inferior and unclean, these traits were now regarded less as the effects of slavery than as a set of characteristics somehow associated with being a Negro. With little opportunity for actual significant contact with Negroes, the white man constructed a Negro fantasy that haunts him to this very day.

The growth of the Negro fantasy in America in the last century is explainable. It was an era of great interest in the romantic and the exotic, and it was not much of an intellectual leap from such interest to a morbid belief in the strange and sinister qualities of unknown groups. There were also the first draughts of the heady wine of theoretical racism that was to become the formal mystique of whole nations in our times. Nor must we omit the fact that this was a relatively young and isolated nation, rather timid in its thinking on international matters. In a society genuinely damaged by the after-effects of slavery, this increasingly unrealistic and fictitious view of the Negro constituted the core of the nation's racial attitude.

The tragedies of slavery scarred the Negro terribly. Personal development, family life, ambitions and expectations would be retarded for generations after the evil institution had been struck down.[4] As the social conditions of other Americans, immigrant and native, improved, the disparity between the sons of freedom and the children of slavery, who were now stepchildren of freedom, became more obvious. The privations and failures needed an explanation. In a nation which for many decades viewed success as the work of God and failure as the mark of sin, according to the Calvinist ethic, the Negro afflictions could be easily attributed to a mysterious moral fault, a flaw in the soul of the Negro.

Thus a view became common that harked back to slavery and had to be referred to slavery to be understood. It was a view that was composed of old fears and rationalized explanations. Fears of slaves and freed slaves, fears of the unknown. Rationalized explanations of privation and ignorance and wild license. This was the common stone of the walls of prejudice and segregation.

There was in addition to the *post facto* judgments of the significance of slavery, the presence of poverty among the Negroes. Our country has been keenly attentive to material gain. The American way of life is founded on material sufficiency. For an ethnic group to be set apart from this tradition of acquisitiveness was a strange thing. It required explanation. Why were Negroes not participants in the great national game of gain and get? What kept them from meriting materialism like everybody else? The answers of exploitation, discriminatory treatment and second-class citizenship were too affronting to self-righteous ears. There had to be some more acceptable reason, some reason in the "nature" of the Negroes themselves. The answer was: Negroes were incapable of managing property intelligently. This explanation became riveted into the popular outlook.

The idea of Negro incompetence in economic and other material matters would have dire consequences in relation to residential property. The Negro neighbor was to be regarded not only as a sinister social influence but also as an active agent of property abuse. When Negroes inhabited a property it became dilapidated and deteriorated in value, thus jeopardizing the value of surrounding residences. This is the way popular belief saw it. Not only did such a view permit property rented by Negroes to be denied repairs, but it tightened the resolve of those who held property to exclude Negroes from it. Indeed it permitted the endorsement of racism by economic interests all over again. In the slave period property was supported and sustained by racial exploitation. In the twentieth century property was withheld from the Negro and used as a sacred symbol he was unworthy to touch.

We shall have reference to this attitude toward the relation of Negroes to property throughout this book. In a nation where social position was based not on family or hereditary codes or a traditional social hierarchy but on the ideal of material success, the fact that the overwhelming majority of Negroes remained poor would have a profound effect on racial views. To the factors of prejudice and privation was added the element of class distinction. Even when the fears of whites for their own safety could be overcome, and when economic gains could be made by the Negro, the venomous snobbery of class notions remained.

Beneath the Mind

The views about Negroes we have been considering thus far have been discussed largely in terms of historical causation.

It remained for modern students of psychology and psychiatry to analyze deeper recesses of character and personality reaction to chart for us the more hidden springs of racial antagonism.[5] Practically all of this theoretical exploration of prejudiced behavior has been performed in terms of depth psychology, the dynamic personality definition deriving from the works of such men as Freud, Jung and Adler. Because of this there is a certain amount of ambiguity and contradictory interpretation in the works of analysis. But the light that has been thrown upon individual and group attitudes by this keenly pursued psychological dissection has been brilliant. Approaches to the study of prejudice by evaluation of structure, perception and projection *(of the personality)* have been extremely rewarding.

Some of the finest work in this field has been done by Gordon Allport, whose theory of prejudice permits a multiple approach to the phenomenon of prejudice and its expression in personal behavior and social situations.[6] Allport's theory points toward personality tendencies, rather than fixed traits. These tendencies become activated by various situations. The merit of this theory is that it poses different levels of causation to explain the complexities of racial attitudes in a complicated society.

The studies of John Dollard view prejudice as a product of frustration.[7] The blocking of drives directed at certain goals creates dissatisfaction and frustration. A certain amount of such frustration produces hostility. This hostility may be stored up, or directed toward oneself, or focused upon some substitute target. The social context may favor the direction of such hostility onto minority group members.

Other theories of prejudice relate intergroup tension and hostility to other personality needs of individuals. The need for self-esteem and social status induces some individuals to exploit the representatives of minority groups for the aggrandizement of their psychological wants or the satisfaction of their anxieties. Still other explanations contend that the organization of the personality itself is the key concern. Rigid personalities tend to be authoritarian and aggressive, it is held, and this aggression responds readily to stereotyped minority targets. There is still considerable debate as to whether one or another personality type is prejudice-prone. The debate takes place in a variety of professional journals and clinical articles, but it has great significance for the fields of intergroup relations, education and moral guidance.

Although these studies of personality help greatly to explain the seemingly baseless reactions of people to racial phenomena, much of the work on this subject is highly abstruse. The conclusions about the causes of racial antagonism are not widely known. This is unfortunate. The historical and economic causes of racial hostility are things about which little can be done at this late date. The social experiences producing these factors are behind us to a great extent. The human personality, however, is very much with us, active in its formation and expression. Whatever we can do to guide its development and to overcome dispositions toward prejudice and aggressive behavior should be undertaken energetically. We are indebted to the discoveries and theories of depth psychology, but in a mass society with mass media and regularized channels of personality experience, we should be able to make much more beneficial use of these findings than we have. The cultivation of violence and aggression through the mass media is only mildly reproached in our society, for instance; hence it is not surprising that the hostility it generates has repercussions in the field of race relations.

The utilization of social (as distinguished from individual) psychology to probe racial problems has been of tremendous benefit to progress in intergroup thinking. The opinion of whole groups was the object of interest among pioneers of social science in France. As the studies of sociology and anthropology developed, social psychology became greatly augmented. The peculiar behavior resulting from rumor, fear, panic and crowd conditions, as well as the function of ethnic beliefs in conflict situations, became the material for careful study. The effects of group attitudes and loyalties on both minority and majority groups were gradually catalogued. The works of such men as Muzafer Sherif and Otto Klineberg are landmarks in this field.[8] Books like Hadley Cantril's *The Psychology of Social Movements* are models of social insights.[9]

Economic, social and political currents have been traced by social psychology, including their effects on group relations. The effects of economics on the occurrence of lynching, the reaction of poor-whites to political demagogues or the reaction of Negroes to a charismatic leader are all subjects for the illumination of social psychology.

The formation of a body of social-science knowledge about group psychology has made possible the writing of the history of race relations in a completely new and revealing dimension. Just as valuable has been the benefit to police work, mass communications and intergroup education in dealing with current problems of racial conflict and misunderstanding. In the urban environment, where popular opinion is molded by synthetic information and artificial influences, it is the study of social psychology that has the most immediate value for the preservation of civic peace and the reform of group opinion.

Slums, Crime and Sex

We have reviewed briefly the major sources of the racial hostility that is part of urban life today. Some of the more general conditions of urban development bearing upon race relations opinion were examined in Chapter I. It would be well to look at other features of today's urban life that affect racial attitudes. The social situation in urban centers is unique in the history of individual and group life, and its effects on race relations are likely to be productive of entirely original relationships. Even though such relationships are not evident at this time, the new forces the metropolis has propagated will doubtless result in distinctive patterns.

The association of Negroes with poverty and lower social position in the past has led to their attachment to that grotesque urban social institution, the slum. The slum has been a fixture in urban life since the rise of the industrial cities of the eighteenth century. It has remained a focal point of family misery and social disorganization during the whole course of modern urban development. The slum defied the fervent religious and humanitarian reform efforts of the last century and is apparently holding its own against the welfare state in recent decades. The slum, in addition to being a set of inferior social conditions and standards, is also a picaresque folk world of personal deviation and extreme personality reaction. This is particularly true when the slum becomes the setting for underprivileged and segregated minority group life.

The effects of continuous Negro residence in slum areas upon urban racial attitudes have been manifold.[10] The nonwhite habitation of slums has become as much an urban institution as the slums themselves. All of the social ills endemic to slum areas have served to deepen and ramify the "marks of oppression" inherited by Negroes from slavery and the peonage of Southern share-crop existence. A vicious interpretation of the poverty of Negroes has capitalized upon the obvious privations of slum life to reinforce the argument that Negroes are incapable of property care and economic improvement. The cumulative effect of the prolonged Negro association with the slum has been to impart an image of colored citizens stricken by continuing difficulties. This image has prevented the adoption of the Negro into those bland and serene model American categories, the middle class and the "well-to-do." Whatever the reality of Negro achievement and ability, the image just will not dissolve. In terms of residential life, this means that it is terribly difficult for white residents to conceive of a Negro middle class with middle-class mores and background. The Negro family that exhibits middle-class tastes and choices is consequently viewed with suspicion and suspected of bizarre motives.

Another phase of urban social life with which Negroes have been associated in the city is the realm of criminality. While it is an understood and understandable consequence of social disorganization, the connection between criminal activity and Negro neighborhoods goes beyond the simple dictum that "the poor and unfortunate produce a disproportionate number of criminals." The psychological significance of crimes by non-whites is a major factor in urban race relations. It is true that Negroes have not been identified with the murderous big-time criminal syndicates that are still a ruthless part of our city life. Nor have Negroes been admitted to the nefarious ranks of the "white collar" criminals and "operators," whose grafts and greeds plague the business and financial world. What is distinctive about the problems of Negroes who become law-breakers is the abiding cultural stereotype that becomes activated by the process, and the manner in which the communications media abet distorted reactions to crimes by Negroes.[11]

There are other groups, notably the Irish and the Italians, who have had to offset widespread unfavorable stereotypes about their ability to abide by law. Their battles with the issue are largely in the past. The indictment of these groups, however, was not nearly so persistent historically as has been the indictment of the highly visible Negro. Nor did the indictment of the Irish and the Italian affect so many people simultaneously, as does the imputation of criminality to Negroes as a group today. And while it is true that the press has always tended to sensationalize crime in the United States since the advent of yellow journalism in the last century, the power of today's tabloid press for morbid exaggeration and sensational distortion did not exist in the nineteenth century, nor did the powerful television dramatization.

There has been a deep American folk belief in the criminality of Negroes. It may stem from the fear of slave uprisings or the menace of freed slaves. It may stem from the cultural association of dark color with mystery, evil and sinister portents. Or it may derive simply from beholding the tragic plight of people twisted into rebellion against society by social exclusion and other injustices. This belief has been nurtured by a residential segregation that prevented any real interracial contact. The crimes of Negroes in large cities are mostly robbery and crimes of passion. The carefully organized underworld gangs and syndicates of the big cities have not, as we have noted, been constructed by Negroes. The offenses of Negroes are usually those of individual adults or teen-age vandals and street killers.

The urban press treats these crimes in a manner that tends to magnify them. In the hand-to-mouth minority press there is steady, blatant, wildly headlined coverage of crime. In the metropolitan dailies there is usually very little news of local Negroes in the North. The segregation problems of the South are covered, as are the successes of the Negro elite. But of business and society news, civic affairs and normal Negro activity, there is rarely regular coverage. When Negroes commit rape, murder, mayhem or armed robbery, they are thrust into the "crime sensation" category, particularly if the crimes are against white victims. Thus, when the public does see news about Negroes, it is usually the out-of-context, luridly treated crime news, unaccompanied by even those human interest features that tend to balance the impact of crimes committed by whites.

The attributing of criminality to Negroes as a group is a potent influence in conditioning the minds of whites to look on Negro neighbors as a threat to property and community standards. Like so much similar stereotyped thinking, the "Negro crime" fixation is not amenable to facts. The law-abiding behavior of the great majority of non-whites is dismissed. The criminal deviant is magnified to obsessive prominence. So strong is the distorted view and image that it seldom yields to reasoned argument. Something like a mass therapy is required to exorcise it from public opinion.

Much less has been written about sex as a factor in race relations. In the urban environment sexual thinking has taken a special form. Sex is not only a function of the human organism in urban society, it is a commercially and scientifically exploited stimulus that serves as a means of communication. When critics such as Harvard sociologist Pitirim Sorokin say that we have undergone a sex revolution and we live in a sex-saturated society, this does not mean that actual sexual indulgence has necessarily increased. It does mean that a vulgar eroticism pervades fashion, the graphic media and common cultural expression, so that synthetic evocations and gross references to sex are everywhere. All the arts of display and emphasis utilize sex as an adjunct to commerce and mass communications. The exploitation of sex is not so much that of permitting licentious acts without social control as it is the use of erotica in a sort of commercially contrived psychological game.

How does this characteristic of modern urban life affect race relations? In a sex-saturated society people tend to interpret everything in terms of sex; neckties, automobile designs, weekend weather reports all get a sexy twist. The cultivated atmosphere of phony sex makes it easily applicable to all situations. Hence race relations also become a subject for sexual speculation. Now it is true enough that all things human have some sexual aspects—or, at least, can so be interpreted. But the sexual fantasies bedevilling race relations are more often the result of untrammeled imagination than serious commentary. Indeed, the morbid preoccupation with the subject of interracial marriage and Negro sexual propensities is so widespread in our society that it suggests a serious sickness to any thoughtful observer.

If we relate these facts to the realm of residential life, we can see the intimacy with which the fear of sexual aggression strikes the white man's mind. The home is the focus of so many emotional and sexually significant images that the approach of Negroes to this institution is deeply disturbing to a white mentality steeped in sex and fed on tales of non-white sexual potency and license. No matter what the statistics say about interracial marriage or the normal behavior of Negroes, the mind ridden with sex suggestion looks on the play group, the junior high school and the most casual contact with dire misgivings. This is another of the reasons why white home owners seek to exclude Negroes from their dwelling areas.

With the growth of humanitarian efforts such as the settlement house movement and government social welfare programs, the troubled condition of Negro family life was revealed. High rates of illegitimacy, desertion, disrupted relationships and disorganization were verified in statistical surveys that detailed in cold tabulations the human predicament of tens of thousands. Social scientists and historians could explain these conditions and their origin in the Negro folk society of the South. But the larger society readily assigned these domestic patterns to degeneracy. The popular mind saw these family disorders simply as further evidence of promiscuity, sexual aberration and irresponsible behavior on the part of the Negroes. The wide knowledge of these problems brought about by well-publicized corrective programs and the cost of remedial welfare programs to taxpayers heightened the resentment against the unfortunate victims of the problems.

Residential change arouses racial opinions with a special virulence. When the lines of residential segregation are broken or some influence changes a stalemate or equilibrium between racial groups, then rumor, comment and resolutions reveal the racial lore and information that people have stored up in their minds. For this reason the racially changing neighborhood is a very good place in which to encounter expressions of the many and varied phases of relations between the races. In 1955 the Philadelphia Commission on Human Relations launched an educational program designed to counter some of the most common fears accompanying racial change. The subjects chosen for treatment in the Commission's printed material, sound films and speaking engagements were those which its staff had found to be the overriding concerns of audiences dealt with during fieldwork in racially changing areas. The Commission's material aimed at reassuring citizens about six commonly held fears that troubled race relations at the local level: fear of property loss; fear of loss of social status; fear of interracial marriage; fear of crime; fear of decline in neighborhood standards of property care; fear of being in the minority.

This Philadelphia educational program was something of a prototype in intergroup educational work. It was widely copied by agencies seeking to cope with racial turnover in city neighborhoods. The approach has been criticized by some professional race relations workers as aimed at the wrong targets of local thinking, since it has been found that residents in some areas are not deeply concerned about a decline in standards of property care.[12] The Philadelphia Commission on Human Relations has always contended that this part of its educational program was not a total response to racial change at the neighborhood level.[13] Nevertheless the reasoning and appeals directed at residents of changing areas through this program and similar ones represent a highly important attempt of urban governmental and civic groups to reshape racial opinion on the basis of social facts.

States of Opinion

If we assume that most of the influences previously discussed in this chapter are at work in the mind of the urbanite, we might next consider how these elements of opinion about race combine in community affairs to affect the course of racial movement in the city. What are the varying degrees in which racial opinion is excited in changing residential areas? Trusting that simplification at this point will not do violence to accuracy, we shall now, for purposes of clarity, summarize separately various stages or degrees of local opinion reaction. These classifications are descriptive rather than analytically precise.

Tension Opinion. Racial thinking generally enters this phase in a community where some incident has occurred which poses the threat of racial change. There is no overt violence or vandalism, but there is agitation, threats, or other forms of intimidation. Such racial tension could be documented in the community reaction of the suburb of Deerfield, Illinois, outside Chicago, when a homebuilder proposed to erect an "open occupancy" development which would attract Negroes to the area.[14] The mere threat that a home may be sold to a Negro is enough for the activation of racial suspicions and stereotypes in the minds of most all-white communities. This sort of tension opinion, which arises in an unorganized way largely without leaders, is replete with rumors. The more responsible elements in the community hold out against the fears and conjectures. The opinion is not usually oriented to action, but is rather a vague and impulsive expression of resentment at the prospect of racial change occurring at the local level. Such opinion can be strongly affected by events involving race occurring elsewhere. Thus local crime news, or integration disputes in other states, or even news about Africa may aggravate the tension.

Panic Opinion. This phase of popular reaction is characterized by greater distress than the tension phase. Discussion is more heated, threats are stronger, opinion leads to action— usually indignant physical withdrawal from the scene of the racial change. There is a greater urgency, and hasty moves are made to resolve a situation deemed intolerable. The response is not so much willful as it is distraught. Such must have been the condition produced by the first entry of Negroes into New York's Harlem, described by Robert Weaver.[15] A flighty, nervous, panic psychology has certainly characterized many of the neighborhoods in the urban centers confronted by racial change after World War II. Chicago had a very extensive turnover of racial groups in what seems to have been record time in the 1950's.[16] When opinion is at the panic stage in a neighborhood, there has usually been some actual racial change or unmistakable incident. Not only are fears and suspicions active, but they have been sufficiently stimulated or confirmed to result in the deposition of the ordinary leaders of opinion and recourse to sudden and ill-considered statements or actions, such as the sale of houses or the closing of facilities.

Aggressive Opinion. Openly aggressive reaction generally endorsed by local residents is not common. It can occur when there is a very aggressive leader who induces a combative and pugnacious spirit. This kind of reaction prevails when extremists either have taken actual control of local attitudes or have established leadership of a sufficient number of people un-questionably to dominate the scene. Such was the case in Levit-town, Pennsylvania, in 1957, when local hotheads created the community disorder which followed the move of the first Negro into the sixteen-thousand-home development.[17] This kind of furious response can be made to support boycotts, physical violence and malignant campaigns of harassment and terroriza-tion against Negroes or the friends of Negroes.

Sustained, widely shared hostile opinion opens the way for grave incidents and riotous defiance of law and order. This was the case in the area around the Trumball Park public housing project in Chicago in 1953.[18] In Collins Park, Delaware, in 1959 explosions twice wrecked a house that had been pur-chased by a Negro, and police were initially unable to obtain any information leading to the arrest of those responsible.[19]

In large cities where mentally disturbed persons can be quickly attracted by crowds, widely publicized incidents or other disorders, there is always great danger that the generally expressed hostility of the residents of an area may stimulate the most dangerous kind of insane action on the part of the men-tally ill.

The significance of aggressive opinion and violence will be treated in a separate chapter later in this book.

Diehard Opinion. In some communities racial change has been a constant possibility for a long period of time, and yet it has not actually occurred; it may have been forestalled many times. This is where what might be termed "diehard" opinion prevails. In certain city neighborhoods where a "racial bound-ary" has been drawn, the white residents will defend this line, often defined by a street or a physical barrier, relentlessly. The Negro will not cross the line in any permanent fashion. Diehard opinion will support its mandate with violence, but even more important is its maintenance of abiding hostility and vigilance.

In so-called "ethnic" neighborhoods composed of foreign-language elements, the morale of the ethnic group may depend upon anti-Negro attitudes. There are areas where housing is segregated by the half-block with the limit of non-white extension clearly identified at a certain house halfway along an entire row. In other areas a particular single house or a few houses are consigned to non-white occupancy. This indicates the definiteness of diehard opinion.

Diehard opinion is alert, tough and committed to the opposition of racial change. It can be played upon for purposes of political, religious or ethnic solidarity. It is a ready threat to law and order. Although such opinion is basically defensive in its outlook, exercising a protective racial sovereignty over a piece of territory, it can interpret any number of events as threats to the status quo and move into the offensive. A hit-and-run accident involving a white child and a Negro driver can whip diehard opinion into embittered aggression. The casual parking of a moving-van can produce effects almost as serious. Juvenile gangs sometimes reflect the racial demarcations of such opinion and adopt racial boundaries as the boundaries of juvenile "turf" to be defended against interloping gangs by street wars and treaties.

Defeatist Opinion. When racial change has been going on for some time in an area, the white resident may become demoralized and lose confidence in the area in a slow process of civic subversion. This may be because total racial turnover of the area seems inevitable or because there have been disturbing incidents during the period of racial change. Leaders who have made efforts to stabilize changing areas can become defeatist when their efforts are rebuffed or set back by untoward circumstances. At times the most dejected elements in a changing area will be those once ardent liberals who entered wholeheartedly into the cause of integration and were disillusioned in the process. This kind of opinion can be found also among white families who are unable to move away from racial change. They remain, and adopt an attitude of pessimism toward their situation. The psychological attitudes of white people faced by racial change range widely, but it must be conceded that the white person in our society who assumes a minority position vis-à-vis Negroes does not usually do so with confidence.

The effects of defeatist opinion are deep and far-reaching. It can lead to disorganization of a community and its institutions. It can and does mean a decline in local prestige, services, leadership and vigor. On the personal level it can develop into acute paranoid states of mind and produce individual and family misery. In the broader channels of urban society it can seriously hinder such functions as education, planning and renewal. Having nurtured a bogy in fantasy, the white mentality pays the price of pessimism and morbidity when its dream comes true.

Constructive Opinion. The reaction of the minority group in a community is positive and wholesome in some instances of racial change. There are almost always some individuals or groups who will rise above racial thinking and confront a given change with objectivity and directness.[20] The motivation may be religious, humanitarian or simply enlightened self-interest. This kind of opinion tends to be slow in asserting itself, and all too often it is not well enough represented to be decisive. The effectiveness of such persons or groups depends on the degree of boldness with which they act and the kind of social situation and other media they utilize to bring about desegregation or racial harmony. A conservative church led by a dynamic minister can produce a stalemate in racial matters. One liberal neighborhood leader, however, can turn the entire course of events in a changing neighborhood.

The outlets for the influence of constructive opinion vary widely. In some communities such opinion may be represented only by isolated individuals. In other areas the churches, schools, political organizations and civic institutions may be formally committed to meeting racial situations constructively. To be effective, constructive opinion about race and minority groups must be clearly conceived and prudent in its practical applications. Mere slogans or liberal emotionalism will soon be subverted, for the roots of prejudice are deep and the ancient power of racism can wear down all but the most clearly defined tolerance and good judgment.

Today both politics and "the public morality" have constructed a network of information media to sustain opinion blocs supporting racial amity and equality of treatment. Private organizations such as the National Conference of Christians and Jews, the National Catholic Conference for Interracial Justice, and the Anti-Defamation League of B'nai B'rith issue numerous publications and sponsor many programs to consolidate and direct opinion. Public commissions which sponsor intergroup relations education programs and accompany their law enforcement procedures by educational efforts now exist in most of the nation's large cities and on the state and Federal government levels. Groups like these can exert a strong influence in community life. They have public endorsement and access to the mass media and usually avail themselves of representative community spokesmen. The greatest problem that such groups face, however, is that they have been instituted in a didactic fashion. They did not arise naturally, with widespread popular backing, but were produced as instruments to solve some particular problem and have only now gradually begun to gather support for their objectives.

We should not confine our consideration of race opinion only to the opinion of the white group. It is true that the majority group attitudes present the most vexing obstacles to the development of interracial co-operation and understanding, but the state of Negro opinion is also a highly important factor in the course of racial change. The popular presumption that Negro opinion is largely passive cannot be maintained today in the face of the vigorous expressions of minority group reactions that occur daily. Keeping in mind the fact that we are here concerned with the kinds of opinion that have a bearing on the movement of racial groups in urban areas, we can distinguish several prominent categories of Negro opinion which affect social and residential mobility.

Resignation or *"Uncle Tom" Opinion.* It should not be surprising that within the Negro group there is a strong current of "accommodationist" opinion. This is most notable at two social levels. In the successful conservative circles, it is not so much a question of personal effacement as it is an expression of the caution protective of vested interests. Thus wealthy Negro businessmen or well-to-do publishers refrain from more than a nominal allegiance to the Negro "protest" organizations. Negro politicians at times exercise a paradoxical moderating influence in civil rights matters. At another level, the comfortable wage-earner, the man who has no real interest in civic and social affairs and has a full larder at home, may feel that the counsel of letting well enough alone absolves him from exertion or attention.[21] Most Negroes have had humiliating experiences because of their race. Most have not been able to fight back successfully against the forces of prejudice and discrimination. Many conclude that any such fight is doomed to failure. Therefore, as long as there is no crisis or immediate personal involvement they studiously avoid challenging the terms of the racial status quo set up by the dominant group.

The proportion of the Negro population adhering to "Uncle Tom" patterns of passive thinking varies from city to city. In some metropolitan centers such opinion is definitely out of fashion among Negroes generally, and there is a more assertive spirit abroad. In other areas, lack of education, weak leadership, continuing dependence upon white benefactors and simple poverty induce an almost total passivity.

Gradualism. The philosophy of gradual achievement seems to be the most prevalent opinion influence among Negroes during times of prosperity and normal activity. The conditions or contrasts surrounding progress are not questioned very deeply, as long as there is perceptible progress. Most people seem willing to accept the premise that progress is gradual for everybody. The rate of progress is not criticized, perhaps, because many Negroes have not developed clear standards of comparison or high aspirations.

It is within the framework of this type of opinion that residential segregation finds its practical acceptance. There is also acceptance of racial distinctions and the milder forms of discrimination. This opinion finds its outlet in the institutions, clubs, and other organizations within the segregated Negro community. Groups promoting civic betterment, scholarships for good students and job-finding or job-training programs find their strongest support among those subscribing to the doctrine of avoiding conflict and fostering gradual improvement. Although this opinion is not greatly different from "Uncle Tom" opinion, there is between the two outlooks this distinction: the "Uncle Tom" takes whatever treatment is accorded him; the gradualist expects and works for the improvement and treatment that he believes he merits.

Militant Opinion. Under the impact of oppression and unjust treatment the Negro protest movement has developed in a slowly ascending curve. The opinion behind it is that of an elite, informed and alert to the challenges that racism and segregation present. If at times such opinion is strident in its expression, or doctrinaire, or even vindictive, it is merely following the classic line of protest crusades that has characterized peasant revolts, land movements and trade unionism. Militant Negro opinion has a variety of sounding boards. National civil rights organizations shape their policy according to its dictates. It supports legal and non-violent approaches to racial problems. Very, very rarely has it condoned or sympathized with violent measures, although the provocation has frequently been extreme. Tactically, the most effective elements of this opinion group have associated themselves with programs or individual efforts to defy segregation or overcome racial restrictions. The effort of "pioneer" families to obtain dwellings in restricted all-white areas often brings such groups as the NAACP, the Committee on Racial Equality and a great many less well-organized groups to their assistance. Since they are vehicles of elite opinion, these groups have seldom been able to bring to bear enough mass support to break the residential segregation system. Instead they have waged a legal war of attrition and criticism against the segregation process.

When it is encountered at the local level or in some crisis situation, militant Negro opinion acts as a counter to diehard white opposition. The opinion that leads to a solution of the particular problem in question is usually more moderate and widely shared. Militant opinion makes possible a solution, however, by raising the issue and exerting pressure for change. The protagonists of militancy and sharp measures to undercut segregation advance two strong arguments for their approach. One is that when dealing with questions of human and civil rights there should be no compromise, for compromise on such issues is a betrayal of moral and legal principles that have been dearly bought and fostered in our society. A second strong argument for militancy is that the racial problem is so long-standing, so resistant to compromise solution, that progress toward full equality can only be made through the most adamant assertion of minority group demands.

The militants in the setting of big-city leadership and competition serve the purpose of keeping the necessity of desegregation alive as an issue in the public mind. This responsibility is heavy and often frustrating, and the temptation to demagoguery is constant. With access to mass media and political influence, militant Negro opinion has broken out of the dialogue it maintained for decades with the white liberal elements, and now appeals directly to the public at large. It may be moving into a period of greater influence in race relations than at any time in the history of Negro life in this country, and it does so with the problem of urban residential segregation squarely before it.

Toward a New Outlook

In order to deal with all of the above phases of racial opinion, numerous educational programs have been devised with the aim of preventing misunderstanding, avoiding hostility between racial and ethnic groups and providing factual information about racial change. These programs often overlap and reinforce one another. Some deal with racial and religious relations in general, others are aimed at resolving problems in employment, the use of community facilities or housing. Many of the programs are under public auspices and are adjuncts to the enforcement of civil rights and fair employment laws. It is frequently asserted that such programs aim less at changing attitudes than at changing practices, although altering a practice without some revision of the intellectual basis for it is hardly conceivable.

Intergroup education programs to influence opinion operate with a variety of tools. Usually, effective programs are staffed by professional specialists in intergroup education, who either carry out the actual program or co-ordinate the activities of volunteers who do so. Public hearings, speakers bureaus, publications, seminars and study plans, volunteer surveys, pledge-signing campaigns, radio and television presentations, picketing and even a process of conversational therapy are used by agencies and organizations to reconstruct racial views and practices. Research and the popularization of academic findings are a major part of the process. At times particular instances of discrimination afford the opportunity for a full-scale debate about discrimination. The treatment of such athletic notables as Jackie Robinson or Olympic swimmer Sammy Lee at the hands of real estate brokers upholding exclusion codes, riots in Levittown, Pennsylvania, or fire deaths in the crowded ghetto tenements of South Chicago periodically spark publicity about the evils of residential segregation.

Programs to offset the opinion which supports segregation work at various levels. Some groups have been very successful in publishing valuable and readable pamphlets and study materials. The Anti-Defamation League of B'nai B'rith and the American Jewish Committee are extremely able in this regard. Another approach is through widespread activities at the neighborhood level involving sustained consultation with local institutions and organizations. The Philadelphia Commission on Human Relations, the Hyde-Park Kenwood Community Association in Chicago and Neighbors, Inc., in Washington, D. C., have programs of this type. An approach that is personalist and more informal emphasizes bringing persons of different races and backgrounds together in a face-to-face situation to stimulate learning and the exchange of views. The Cleveland Commission on Human Relations, Friendship House and the Fellowship House movement have worked with success through such a program. Finally, churches and church-sponsored groups place responsibility directly upon the individual to adopt constructive racial attitudes and to practice fair treatment in the community. The Presbyterian Synods, Catholic Interracial Councils, and the Society of Friends, as well as many other religious organizations, have increasingly brought the moral imperative for interracial justice to bear upon specific problems.

These programs to reshape opinion about race, ethnic groups and the social problems of segregation have gained strength as urban conditions forced more and more debate about racial distinctions. The influence of international criticism of American race relations, the momentum of minority group improvement, our rising educational level, and political considerations have led to an expansion of intergroup education. This, in turn, has greatly changed the general climate of opinion in urban areas outside the South. Urban leadership today speaks carefully about racial issues. The public at large is reserved, at least in public. Strategic opinion groups, such as boards of directors, managers of campaigns and organizations, and publicists, are now willing to think and speak in terms of the verified social facts where such are available, rather than rely entirely on traditional racial views and practices to set forth their positions. It is fortunate that these educational influences have developed during the last two decades, just as Negroes were becoming urbanized. Perhaps they arose in response to the population change. It is equally possible that they represent a logical appurtenance of our democratic society, a necessary invention for a pluralist nation. The great trial of these education media and institutions is still ahead. They have slowed down the urban segregation process; they have not stopped it. Their task is to undermine its basis in popular opinion.

It has been well verified that residential proximity between persons of different races in an environment without undue stress produces an improvement in intergroup attitudes.[22] The possibility for sustained contact is growing in our large communities. Thus the effects of good teaching in our school systems and special intergroup relations education programs should be augmented by realistic learning gathered in employment and recreation situations, and, eventually we hope, in increased contact in residential life.

NOTES

1. Nels Anderson, *The Urban Community: A World Perspective*, p. 31.
2. Robert Weaver, *The Negro Ghetto*, p. 359.
3. Charles Abrams, *Forbidden Neighbors*, p. 26.
4. W. E. B. Du Bois in *The Souls of Black Folks* (Chicago, McClurg, 1909) tells of the wretched overcrowding of cabins and the squalor in rural Georgia at the beginning of this century. See p. 140.
5. E. S. Simpson and J. M. Yinger, *Racial and Cultural Minorities* (New York, Harper, 1953). This book provides an excellent summary of this development in Part 1 of its text.
6. "Prejudice: a Problem in Psychological and Social Causation," *Journal of Social Issues,* November 1950.
7. "Hostility and Fear in Social Life," *Social Forces,* October 1937, p. 18. See also his *Caste and Class in a Southern Town* (New Haven, Yale University Press, 1938).
8. M. Sherif, *An Outline of Social Psychology* (New York, Harper, 1948). Otto Klineberg, *Social Psychology* (New York, Holt, 1940).
9. New York, Wiley, 1941.
10. E. Franklin Frazier in *The Negro Family* (Chicago, University of Chicago Press, 1939) tells of the way in which established middle-class Negroes fled from poor Negro migrants arriving in the cities.
11. For an examination of the lopsided picture of non-whites presented in the daily press, see *The Negro in the Philadelphia Press,* a doctoral dissertation by George E. Simpson (University of Pennsylvania, 1936). For evidence that practices of highly selective and distorted reporting of minority affairs in the newspaper have not changed greatly in recent years, see the report on a Seminar for the

Mass Media held by the Philadelphia Commission on Human Relations, 1961.

12. For some of the thinking behind this program see John McDermott and Dennis Clark, "Helping the Panic Neighborhood," *Interracial Review*, August 1955, and Dennis Clark, "Delayed Action Programs in Changing Neighborhoods," *Interracial Review*, January 1958.

13. See Annual Reports of the Philadelphia Commission on Human Relations for a view of the full Housing Program.

14. Marvin Weisbord, "Homes Without Hate," *The Progressive*, January 1961.

15. *The Negro Ghetto*, p. 19.

16. This was true in the Chatham and Hyde Park areas. See Julia H. Abrahamson, *A Neighborhood Finds Itself* (New York, Harper, 1959).

17. See *House and Home*, October 1957.

18. The Chicago Commission on Human Relations, *The Trumball Park Homes Disturbances* (August 1953, June 1955).

19. See *House and Home*, May 1959.

20. Such a case is well illustrated by the fine educational work performed by the civic and religious groups in Levittown, New Jersey, in 1959 and 1960, prior to the entry of the first Negro families. The work was reported by the Burlington County Human Relations Commission.

21. Shelton Granger, "A View of Negro Self-Segregation," *Journal of the National Association of Intergroup Relations Officials*, May 1960. "The group became ingrown. A review of some of the problems of this ingrown community is not a happy one. Crime rate is out of proportion to the population. The very high incidence of illegitimacy and crimes of assault have long led to interesting sociological and psychological speculations about 'Negro Personality.' Educators report irrefutable evidence that Negro children represent the greater proportionate majority of slow learners and poor readers, and lack interest in acquiring skills and tools for effectively participating in a competitive industrial society. The background of the Negro family is still too largely matriarchal, with loose ties and insufficient patterns for helping boys achieve their status as males so that they may function more adequately in the masculine role they are expected to fulfill. Most of the business could function in only

the Negro area—they lack perpetuity, and it is not likely that they would survive in a freely competitive economy. The problems of the unchurched and unreached youth are significant ones. With the exception of a few core groups, Negro organizations function largely for social purposes. The differences in the structure of community groups among white and Negro people is in the strong absence of paralleling social classes. Among the white group there is a substantial upper class, a very large middle class and a smaller lower class. Among Negroes there is relatively no aristocracy or upper class, a growing but relatively small middle class, and a vast lower class. The problems of the Negro are the problems of Second-Class Citizenship."

22. See, for instance, The Connecticut Commission on Civil Rights, *Private Interracial Neighborhoods in Connecticut* (1959); Hans Speiegel, "Tenants' Intergroup Attitudes in a Public Housing Project," *Phylon,* Spring 1960; M. Deutsch and M. E. Collins, *Interracial Housing* (Minneapolis, University of Minnesota Press, 1951).

4

The Housing Industry—
Unfree Enterprise

THE HISTORY of homebuilding and real estate marketing has been turbulent. Not only has competition been intense and speculation rife, but professional organization has lagged and the economics of the housing market have been erratic.[1] The use of the word "industry" to designate the business networks that transfer and finance real estate is questionable. The business elements which produce and market dwellings form a rather haphazard structure of interlocking interests rather than an industry in any accurate sense of the word. The business of producing and exchanging residential property goes on, however, and with it the ordination of residential racial patterns.

Homebuilding and real estate brokerage have traditionally been easy business areas to enter. As one builder put it, "Anybody who has a wheelbarrow and who can get his hands on some land is a homebuilder." A great deal of capital has not generally been required. It is not uncommon for a sizable portion of the homebuilding companies in an area to be made up of men who began as odd-job carpenters, stonemasons, bricklayers, or even laborers. This speaks well for American initiative, but there seems to be no reasonable expectation that such self-made men, who have had to forego higher education, should be capable of dealing with the complexities of the residential segregation problem. The relative ease with which homebuilding operations can be set up has also meant that profiteers and speculators can become part of this business rather easily.[2] Some letterhead, a telephone, and access to plots of land and construction contractors has made many fortunes in the building business. Real estate brokers are licensed by the states, and there are usually some modest educational requirements in the form of a test or examination for license applicants. Real estate salesmen are vaguely regulated in most states. The real estate field is highly complicated and has traditionally been an arena for exploitation and sharp practice.

The Middlemen

For years efforts have been made to bring more stability and better business practices into the real estate and building field. The National Association of Home Builders was organized only in the 1940's. It now embraces as affiliates over a thousand local associations. The National Association of Real Estate Boards is of much more venerable age, having been formed in 1908. These organizations, however, are liaisons of convenience rather than effective regulatory bodies. They have codes of ethics that are well-meant, but ambiguous and highly generalized. Censure is seldom invoked for breaches of the codes as a practical matter. The local real estate boards, now established for more than half a century, have helped shape legislation and property codes at the local and state levels. The national associations have been potent Washington lobbyists. As stabilizing influences, these organizations have established a minimum of order, but it is rather the changing technology of homebuilding and the influence of government programs that are imposing new, more rational construction and business procedures. Mass-production homebuilding, government-insured mortgages requiring appraisals, credit scrutiny, minimum property standards, etc., have dictated basic requirements that must be met. These factors, plus growing communication and a sense of common involvement, have set a trend toward steadier conduct in the housing field. *House and Home,* the big and informative magazine of the housing field, reflects this trend, as do the joint conferences on mortgage problems, new techniques and urban renewal that now occur frequently.[3]

A further characteristic of the housing "industry" is that the practitioners who develop and sell real estate are basically intermediaries. They do not produce a product in the same sense as fabricators in other sections of the economy. Homebuilders serve as co-ordinators for the services of a host of tradesmen, artisans and material suppliers. The joint product is a house, usually built without benefit of an architect and often very crude in construction. Thus the builder is more a director of traffic in skills than a manufacturer. The real estate broker is even more clearly a functionary, an adjunct to the actual development and improvement of property. The broker and real estate manager are middlemen. They may be strategically placed, but they are largely dependent upon others for the properties and conditions by which to conduct their business. Again, it must be noted that housing economics have been subject to violent fluctuations, and this has contributed to the unsteady stance of those engaged in the field.

Another important feature of real estate as a business is that it is still controlled to an amazing extent by white personnel. There are Negro real estate brokers, and some large cities may have several dozen. But Negro brokers are usually excluded from real estate boards, and their operations are almost always confined to the segregated areas, where housing is likely to be of poor quality and low value. Some real estate boards have a token Negro membership, but even this is rare. Despite the fact that a few Negroes have been able to enter the real estate brokerage business, they are excluded from an active role in the affairs of the organizations pertaining to that business.[4] The all-white character of the industry has deep significance in relation to residential segregation. The inadequacy of Negro representation in the real estate field has obviously served to entrench the mentality which produces discriminatory restrictions. The white membership in industry circles is more than symbolic. It is a condition for the conduct of real estate activity along racist lines.

As can be seen from this description of the homebuilding and real estate elements of the housing industry, there is no strong rationale in the field. Operations are a series of opportunities and risks. The property owner owes little allegiance to the real estate broker. There is no love lost between subcontractor and builder. All elements, however, can quickly reach agreement that racial matters represent one more source of risk where there are already countless variable and unknown factors. Hence a tightly held attitude of half-nervous, half-combative antipathy toward racial matters prevails.

The Money Men

The financial interests that provide construction loans, mortgage loans, insurance and collateral for residential development and exchange are quite different in external characteristics from the housing purveyors we have been describing. The personnel and management of financial institutions are more formally educated, more secure and less subject to economic hazard than the homebuilder and real estate broker. They have the solidity of institutions to support them. The directors of financial institutions generally have a more comprehensive picture of the extent of racial change than do real estate brokers or homebuilders. The connections of financial institutions with a variety of businesses, levels of community activity and locations usually afford a broad view of racial distribution and conditions. It is possible for the financier at least to see the general course of racial change in an urban area, even if the institution itself makes no move to adjust its practices or those of the community to the change. Because of this extensive view of local problems, even though it is a view limited to economics, the responsibility of financial institutions is grave. If they rigidly oppose equality of opportunity and the improvement of circumstances for the minorities in the population, their culpability is great.

There is nothing that quenches radicalism more quickly than the responsibility of handling other people's money. It is paradoxical that financial institutions, which must invest their funds on a universal condition of economic risk, are keenly sensitive to the risk of unpredictable events. It is apparent that mortgage lending institutions have changed their estimation of the Negro as a lending risk. The post-war generation of Negro home buyers has frequently been able to obtain mortgage funds, though these funds have been granted under conditions that have, in effect, caused Negroes to pay a differential for their mortgages because of the age and location of the houses they have purchased.[5] The Commission of Race and Housing studies show that Negroes have been obtaining mortgage loans in segregated areas. Exceptions to this now rather general state of mortgage availability for segregated housing are in those broad belts of depressed neighborhoods in the core areas of the large cities. Moreover, the lending for segregated purchase is usually conducted under conventional terms that are far from lenient. In racially changing neighborhoods, mortgage loans are withheld from the initial buyers, "until the trend is clear."[6] In all-white areas it is practically impossible for a Negro to purchase a house and obtain a mortgage from regular sources. The liberalization of financial attitudes which makes possible loans to minorities who are subject to the double misfortune of lower economic capacity and discrimination is something of an improvement. It is partially accounted for by the improving status of the minority groups in question.

Negro home buyers may have gained some access to mortgage funds, but basically the controls are still set against the making of mortgage loans to Negroes in areas moving toward desegregation. Loans to Negroes in all-white areas, or even in areas where the whites are still not "threatened" by current change, are, as we have noted, taboo. The pressures of financial conservatism, investor influence and widespread prejudice make such lending highly disturbing for banks and mortgage companies. As the author of *Residence and Race,* Davis McEntire, remarks, "Liberal credit to buy segregated housing is not an unmixed blessing."[7] Mortgage credit extended to Negro families has made it possible for them to buy themselves deeply into the segregation of the central city areas.[8] Nothing could have served better to reinforce housing segregation. At the same time, it is undeniable that the property purchases of minority families have taken them as a group out of an economic limbo and into the market place, where their buying power will be increasingly asserted.

Unlike the homebuilding and realtor groups, the men of the financial institutions have been traditionally allied with the key business and power elements of the urban community, having easy relationships with the top decision-makers in the industrial

city. Because of this fact, perhaps, the role of the financial fraternity in pandering to racial prejudice and doing business on
a double standard is the more culpable. It is obvious, however,
that financiers work within the social opinions and circumstances of their communities. Their power is great partly because its exercise is usually marked by caution and conservatism. In addition, those who have any searching contact with
the personal views of bankers know that despite their educational and other advantages they can hold social ideas as crude
and as fatuous as those of any other professional clique.

The real estate, homebuilding and financing groups mingle
within that web of contracts and dealings that is woven by the
influential forces of supply and demand. With respect to the
minority population, however, this market web has been woven
by traditions that have begrudged supply and ensured an en-
feebled demand. There are many variables involved in the
special market fabric woven around minority housing needs.
An examination of some of the more important market factors
applying to minority housing will reveal how the special social
characteristics of minorities have interacted with urban real
estate practices to produce an intensification of housing segregation.

Negroes: The Phantom Market

Historically, Negroes and other minorities have constituted
a special real estate problem.[9] Because of their poverty these
groups have been ignored in the ordinary advertising, promo-
tional and other selling efforts directed at the other segments
of the public. Multi-color ads of sleek new kitchens in modern
homes do not have pert Negro housewives in them. Negroes
are not urged to "visit our wonderful new space-age sample

house, when you are out driving next Sunday." Their business is not sought in the new house market or in that portion of the old house market located in attractive, well-equipped residential areas. Their patronage is fostered only for the housing that white families no longer find attractive. In smaller cities it may be unusual to find any exception to this condition. In the large cities it is in the slums that the only real competition for non-white patronage exists. The competition expires, of course, at the very bottom of the economic scale, where housing need does not permit much choice. At this point the minority member in the slum must take whatever is offered him.

In general, the marketing of housing to minorities is a reverse of the regular real estate process. In the market for whites the selling effort is pointed upward, and toward the more able buyer group. In the market for minorities the selling effort is pointed down and capitalizes on the distress of the least able clients.

If we keep in mind this historical pattern of real estate treatment of the minority market, it will be easier for us to understand what has happened in the large urban centers since World War II. The principles of the real estate market with respect to minorities in the past have been: (a) the minority, because of its poverty, cannot be economically served by the regular market; (b) the minority market does not merit sales effort; (c) only those residences that are unattractive to whites should be allotted to the minority market; and (d) minorities are fair game for exploitation in the worst residential areas.

Since the great migrations and the population boom of the post-war years, a new set of market factors has come into play. The wartime housing shortages fell with particular severity upon the urban Negro. Increased buying power on his part activated his demand for post-war relief from these shortages. Similar, but less urgent, factors promoted the exodus of whites to the mushrooming suburbs. Negroes "filled in" neighborhoods that white vacated, and even hastened the exodus of whites by their presence. Negroes have in some cities been able to abandon some of the worst of the residential trash, as is revealed in the high vacancy rates for urban centers in 1960. As mortgage money became much scarcer and more expensive in the late 1950's, the outward rush of Negro demand was spending itself. The scarcity of mortgage funds made further penetration of good residential areas more and more difficult. Thus the expansion of the Negro areas tapered off in one city after another.

The advent of mass homebuilding in the suburbs popularized a long-standing fetish in American residential life. Suburbia made accessible for millions of white families a social status related to single houses on separate lots that has been part of the real estate market since the early part of this century.[10] This newly found "status housing" deepened the feeling of these whites against contact with Negroes, who still carried the stigma of lower-class status.[11] The promotion and sales campaigns of the mass builders were premised upon this popularized status symbolism. Selling brochures alluded to "homes of distinction" and used sales slogans keyed to status images and the evocation of "solid domestic comfort" and the "gracious living for successful modern families." This status-selling mania on a mass basis made white middle-class exclusiveness a reality for millions of former working-class families. What was new was not the status-huckstering process, but the implementation of status as a real fixture of the vast new suburban housing areas for thousands who were reaching the middle class for the first time.

The New Negro

The Negro population in the housing market of the 1950's and 1960's was undergoing changes also. The American folk symbol of the status-laden dwelling was beginning to affect the elite elements of the Negro population despite the fact that appeals to them were censored out of the marketing process. However, this demand for new housing on the part of Negroes was a marginal thing, no matter how significant it would be for the future. The traditional patterns of retarded Negro housing demand still prevailed.[12] This retardation was part of the general cultural lag plaguing the minority population. Economically successful Negroes often preferred old established middle-class areas because of the prestige attached to them. The lure of the suburbs, apart from the fact that it would be bitterly illusory for them, was not so strong. The more conservative taste of the Negro home buyer was not attracted by suburban sleekness. This was in part, of course, a natural result of the fact that no sales effort had been focused on conditioning the group toward suburbia.

There also remained the different pattern of expenditures for housing between whites and Negroes. Except in some slum situations where exploitation forced a high level of rent, Negroes tended to spend a smaller proportion of their income for rent than did whites. This was partly a reflection of poverty and of long-standing mores. It was an outgrowth of the peculiar economic and family history of Negroes.[13]

Another factor in the market behavior of Negroes in the last two decades has been a high mobility rate. Paradoxically, while whites are more free to move, it is Negroes who have had to do more moving. The movements from farm to city and from slums to tolerable housing areas have been the basic sources of this Negro mobility. A third force, however, has been family disorganization. In the older, segregated neighborhoods, the trials of families who have had to change dwellings because of the unemployment or desertion of a wage earner and other kinds of instability have intensified the cycle of housing exchange. This mobility due to social disorganization is a strong factor in racial attitudes. In the more settled city neighborhood the white occupants are horrified by the prospect of such disruptive mobility and see it as something inherently connected with all levels of the Negro population. They are most urgent and intimidating in their demands upon real estate brokers and managers not to permit the phenomenon to enter their area.

Thus to the fundamental racial attitudes and practices of the professional groups in the housing market have been added the peculiar market forces circumscribing minority housing choices. Highly selective mortgage lending, the power of status taboos relating to housing, retarded housing tastes and expenditures of minority families and high mobility rates—these have been important factors in the housing market acting to preserve segregation practices.

Having described in a brief fashion the social posture of the major elements of the housing industry, and having sketched some of the major market forces that influence the residential movement of minority families, we must now look at the actual position of the man who rents or sells housing when he is faced by the immediate prospect of racial change. There are a number of influences that press in upon the real estate broker and the homebuilder when the minority client presents himself. The influences either dictate an outright act of unfair discrimination or so paralyze the businessman that he becomes the tool of segregation proponents.

Pressures for Restriction

What are the influences that impinge upon the purveyor of housing when he is confronted by the prospect of complicity with racial change? The following are the most potent ones:

Business Psychology. The broker or builder is in the full tradition of doctrinaire free enterprise. In a business field that is still rather easily entered, with high priority on personal drive and keen competition, the slogans of free enterprise still have a distinctively appealing ring, despite the contradiction of government intervention all through the housing business. One of the maxims of the free and untrammeled businessman is that he is not a woolly-headed sociologist. The broker or builder disclaims the social viewpoint.[14] He contends that he is a businessman, acting upon business principles for profit. He is not as a businessman concerned with social crusades or improvements. He is too busy balancing the books to work out ways of expanding housing opportunity for minority families, with all the complexities that this would entail.

The businessman tends to eschew responsibility for any part in segregation. He often proclaims himself a neutral agent, a tool of the public, responsive to the public's needs. He sees the responsibility for inducing racial tolerance and harmony as belonging to churches and educational groups. He has no direct role to play.

This mentality exempts him from direct participation in attempts to promote desegregation or change discrimination practices in the market. It is a powerful factor. Groups working for housing desegregation often decry this business outlook or point out its crude contradictions, but it is real and deeply rooted in business circles. It may be a shibboleth for some, but for others it is a sincerely held canon of business ethics. It acts to dispense the broker and the homebuilder from responsibility for the segregation problem.

Personal Prejudice.   Despite the businessman's profession of innocence and freedom from guile in racial matters, even a casual inquiry reveals that the personal racial outlook and attitudes of businessmen are freely exerted in business situations.[15] Not only is the informal speech at real estate luncheons or building conferences rich in the vocabulary of prejudice, but there are many verified instances in which brokers or builders have imposed their racial views on white clients whose own attitudes were liberal. Banking officials and appraisers, while they are more remote from the sales and rental contacts, are no less human and subject to our twisted racial tradition. There are, of course, many men in the housing business who are free of racial antipathy, but they have not set the business practices inherited from the past, nor can they outweigh the more general mentality of racial suspicion and prejudice among those in the field.

Business Retaliation.   The code of racial restriction has been current so long in housing circles that to break it is to be branded as a renegade. The builder who would do so would find it almost impossible to buy land for his next development.[16] The broker who would permit Negro purchase in an all-white area would find himself bereft of shared commissions or clients referred from other brokers. This is no fiction.[17] Partisans of desegregation who deny or try to minimize the predicament of the businessman who defies racial taboos are simply blind to reality. For a real estate broker to "break a block" by introducing the first Negro buyer or renter in some areas means immediate and thorough business ostracism. In a divided and competitive field such as housing, this is one principle that can be agreed to: do not violate the racial code.

It has been true that brokers will by agreement alter racial distribution. Builders can and have built for Negro buyers on marginal land or in sparsely settled areas, but this is not the same as introducing Negroes into those sections of the urban terrain consecrated by tradition and preserved by practice for white occupancy. In Florida a broker who violated the restrictive code was expelled from the real estate board. In Philadelphia builders testified that selling to Negroes would make it impossible for them to continue in business. Business retaliation is indeed real, and it is an ever present consideration to those who might be tempted to break with local restrictive practices.

Reaction of Clients.   The tenant and the home buyer can be manipulated in a general fashion by the businessman. Their housing tastes can be shaped on a long-term basis. Their consent can be evoked to some change that is cautiously introduced. But the real estate broker or manager is clearly subject to the displeasure of his clients.[18] In the matter of racial change, this displeasure can have a disastrous power. Most businessmen work on margins. After their liabilities are met, the remaining margin of income is their profit. A man need not lose 80% of his business and assets to be economically crippled. If he loses 2%, it can slice away the expected profit margin which he may have counted on in two years of patient planning. If involving himself in the affairs of Negroes would deprive him of that critical 2% of his business by diverting white clients from his office, the businessman becomes extremely cautious.

Real estate brokers who have sold to Negroes, or even been rumored to be thinking about sales to Negroes, in restricted areas have been deluged by phone calls. White clients shun their services, in some cases almost totally cutting off business. One broker in San Francisco lost $2,000 in commissions in a short time, after having his name appear on a house sold to a non-white family.[19] Threats of bodily harm to brokers and builders because of sales to Negroes have been common. This kind of reaction among a businessman's clientele is bound to make him deeply suspicious of any involvement with racial change. The exceptions are, of course, those brokers who specialize in meeting the needs of minority families, and these usually have scant prestige with the white public.

The convergence of these pressures hostile to racial desegregation practically immobilizes the real estate broker or builder. His personal predicament can be excruciating. There is sworn testimony to the case of a sales agent at a new housing development who hid in a garage rather than face a prospective Negro buyer at the site.[20] Salesmen at sample houses have displayed wildly distorted judgment in dealing with Negro prospects and come to the verge of tears because they are so much intimidated by the presence of Negro prospects.[21] In Grosse Pointe, Michigan, real estate brokers constructed the most weird and complex system of scoring and rating prospects in order to defend the all-white character of this exclusive suburb.[22]

Lest we indulge in undue sympathy for the businessmen caught in the vortex of this system, we should remember who its real victims are. Businessmen are adequately equipped to defend their own interests. But minority families in overwhelming numbers who are the direct victims of discrimination are innocent of offense and without resources, in need of relief from long-standing inadequacies in housing and subject to unjust treatment in many other areas of life. American private enterprise has many blots upon its record of great achievement. It bitterly opposed labor organization, it ignored social welfare in many obvious cases, and it heedlessly exploited natural resources without regard to the future. Its treatment of minorities in the housing market, however, stands as one of the most outrageous and sustained records of failure of business ethic and personal hypocrisy in our social history.

New Forces

The members of the housing industry have in recent years been subjected to rising pressures from groups opposed to discrimination. These groups have developed a number of techniques for inducing real estate brokers and builders to abandon racial restrictions. The social action committees of the Lutheran Church have sponsored seminars for key men in the housing field. Catholic groups have conducted a broad campaign aimed at changing practices. One Catholic Bishop in Rhode Island personally exerted his influence to alter racial restrictions so that relocation of Negro families could proceed.[23] As we have noted, the Greater Minneapolis Interfaith Housing Committee works to induce white families to sell homes freely to qualified Negroes, and Friends Suburban Housing in Philadelphia operates a real estate office that brings willing white sellers and Negro buyers together in suburban areas. These groups are all very small as yet. The educational work they do, however, is growing and raising questions in the public's mind about the old doctrines of exclusion and restriction.

Of even greater importance is the influence of politics and government non-discrimination policies. Negroes and other minorities unite in politics to have non-discrimination laws adopted. "Fair housing laws," as they are called, now exist in ten states, covering various portions of the housing market. These laws have been upheld by the courts.[24] They lend the prestige of public policy to non-discrimination and make respectable and legally desirable the abandonment of unfair restrictions. Many jurisdictions as well as the Federal Government require that various types of housing built with redevelopment aid be open to all, without restriction based on race, religion or national origin.

The political power of minority groups is growing. The concept of government protection of citizens against arbitrary discrimination is being further clarified every day. Fair housing laws have been proved legally sound. They may not yet represent a means of bringing widespread desegregation in numerical terms, but they do set the precedents and produce the climate for the eventual dispersion of qualified minority families throughout a free housing market.

Another force that will make the position of the broker and builder who upholds restrictions increasingly untenable is the growing economic capability of minority families. A lack of qualified buyers can no longer serve as an excuse for ignoring minority housing needs. Studies of home purchase in various areas bear this out.[25] This increases the possibility that minority families will obtain the houses they want through the operation of a fair housing law or through "front" purchasers who will resell to them. Even more important, it increases the prospect that some one builder or broker, perhaps during periods of slack housing turnover, will build for or market to minority families. This would lead others to do the same rather than forego the chance of ready profits. In times of economic pinch, the minority market may look more and more attractive to housing operators. Whether or not this event is likely, it cannot be denied that economic wherewithal on the part of Negroes and others imperils the discrimination system.

Thus the housing industry is not only subject to highly vexatious internal problems arising from the maintenance of discrimination practices, but it is also faced by changes in the moral, legal and economic climate that are bringing greater long-term pressure on the industry.

White Knights

In an industry as large as that of the construction field there are bound to be mavericks in many senses of the word. Some of the mavericks in the housing field have been those who attempted to market homes to Negroes on a non-discriminatory basis. One of the earliest adventures in this direction was that of St. Louis homebuilder Charles Vatterott. As a Catholic, Vatterott was acutely conscious of the injustice of the restrictive practices he encountered in business. He built a few houses where he could for Negroes, finding it difficult to avoid building on a segregated basis.

George and Eunice Grier found a hundred privately developed interracial communities through the nation in the late 1950's.[26] Some of these were the result of activity by groups such as the American Friends Service Committee, The Urban League and the United Auto Workers. Open occupancy laws applying to any housing built on redevelopment land were influential in some cases. In the overwhelming number of cases, however, there was some factor attached to the development that enabled it to be built and operated in a fashion untypical of the general market procedures. Sometimes there was a special market of a very limited nature that could be profitably served. Backing by influential benevolent groups helped to exempt some developments from the restrictions. In rare instances, builders could defy the prevailing discrimination because they themselves were persons of exceptional ability and initiative, far above the average businessman. Joseph Eichler, builder of lovely homes in the San Francisco area, is such a man. Eichler defied the prevailing restrictions, resigned from the homebuilders association and made headlines with his endorsement of open occupancy.[27] Morris Milgram of Modern

Community Developers, based in Princeton, New Jersey, is another such man. Milgram has built several integrated communities at various price levels. To do so, he has developed a whole national network of support and financial aid for his corporation.

The successes of the rare maverick builder or broker who abandons racial restrictions are usually conditioned by some influence that makes their venture different from the ordinary building or selling operation. Homebuilders and real estate brokers are unconvinced that integrated communities can be sold except in special circumstances. An extended selling period, specially trained sales staff, co-operative mortgage sources and other safeguards are deemed necessary to withstand the buyer resistance and other problems attending business on a non-segregated basis.

The exploits of the mavericks have been heartening. They prove that dedication to justice and zeal for decent practices can overcome tremendous obstacles. Those who rent and sell without discrimination are the thin end of the wedge of large-scale change which will ultimately make housing without unfair restrictions the norm of the market. However, it cannot be said that the mavericks have as yet made a real dent in the prevailing system. In the disputes as to whether their developments have been typical, economical or stable, the lesson they sought to convey to businessmen in the field has been lost. Their testimony to the fact that a combination of idealism and ingenuity on the part of business can make an effective beginning in the removal of unfair housing barriers in a practical way has been confused and dismissed by the cynicism and racial thinking traditional in the housing field.

The attitude of housing businessmen toward those trying to promote integrated communities is one of resentment. They are viewed as either misguided subversives or radical "social work" visionaries. Friends Suburban Housing, the private real estate corporation whose activities we have already mentioned, has been one of the most active non-discrimination groups set up on a business basis. This organization, developed largely by Quakers, has had to hire specially qualified brokers to handle its transactions. Dealing through local brokers has been almost impossible. Acquiring homes repossessed by the FHA and the VA for resale on a non-discrimination basis has been extremely difficult for this group, despite the fact the FHA and the VA are clearly committed by Federal regulation to handling such properties without restrictions. This is typical of the problems such groups face. The traditional practices hem them in on every side.

Toward Solutions

One of the most glaring contradictions in the housing field has been produced by the reliance of its operators at every level on government aid. Loud professions of devotion to free enterprise have not kept builders and lenders from availing themselves freely of the mortgage insurance programs that have been so instrumental in promoting home ownership in this country. The Federal programs that began as emergency measures during the depression decade of the 1930's became permanent stabilizers of the housing economy. They were embraced —indeed, some would say kidnapped and held hostage—by the housing industry.[28] While industry circles have consistently seen "socialism" in the public housing program of low-rent units for low-income families, no such scruples have been popularly voiced about the vast VA and FHA programs. The pervasion of the private housing industry by public assistance in the form of mortgage insurance, minimum construction standards and down-payment requirements has created great public leverage upon construction and home-marketing activities. Government intervention in favor of non-discrimination from the Federal level has been increasing.

The flourishing works of urban renewal are being carried out largely in minority-occupied areas. The United States Civil Rights Commission has recommended that minorities be represented at every stage of renewal planning and development.[29] Relocation housing must be offered on a non-discrimination basis. Legal safeguards against discrimination in redeveloped and renewed facilities are being extended. As private enterprise finds renewal projects more and more attractive, the provisions for non-discrimination will constitute less of a problem.

The prospect is for more government intervention rather than less in years to come. Residential construction and renewal both at the reviving centers and at the expanding edges of the cities will require government co-ordination, subsidies or assistance. The increased importance of city planning in the comprehensive sense and the broad Federal concern for urban problems will also bring more emphasis on consistency of policy in government circles with respect to racial problems. This government influence holds the best promise for breaking the deadlock of discrimination.

There have been suggestions that the industry should try to find its own gradual solution to the discrimination dilemma. One of the strongest proponents of industry responsibility has been John A. McDermott, who held various positions with local and Federal government intergroup relations agencies. James H. Scheuer of the Bowery Savings Bank has been a strong voice urging private business to begin setting its house in order. Chester Rapkin of the Institute of Urban Studies at the University of Pennsylvania even devised an insurance scheme to defray any losses that might be incurred by homebuilders in effecting desegregation, but the scheme was very coolly received by both private and public commentators.

Some few business spokesmen believe that the growth of economic pressure by minority families and very long-range trends in public opinion will slowly solve the problem of restrictions. The tempo of civil rights advances will hardly permit this kind of leisurely evolution. Elimination of restrictions on residential mobility are long overdue. Employment and educational improvements make the residential situation increasingly intolerable. The breakdown of the housing segregation system will come in the next decade. The change will not be total, but it will be decisive.

The private housing industry has shown itself to be highly skeptical of experimental solutions. In the last fifteen years it has all but proved itself incapable of breaking the patterns of restriction. Reform will not come from within the private echelons of the housing field. The lever for breaking the patterns will be government influence. Fair housing laws at the state and local level and regulations banning discrimination in Federally aided mortgage and renewal programs will make discrimination too much of a legal risk for a substantial number of lenders, builders and brokers. The alertness of Negroes in urban life, whose political significance is growing, will insure that these levers are not mere symbols. All the legal, economic and social developments point in this direction. No relief is in sight other than this kind of government influence that will form a counterforce to the inertia and paralysis of the industry itself. There may be grave misgivings in some circles about the intrusion of government into the process of property transfer in outlawing ethnic restrictions, but no responsible or effective alternative has been suggested.

The private business elements of the housing field, as we have said, represent a sphere of enterprise more illustrative of democracy than many other parts of our economy. The decentralized nature of the field, the ease of entry and low-capitalization required, the private and personal nature of the product—the house—all permit considerable attachment to human feelings and dispositions. But like many other parts of American society, the housing industry has failed to act with responsibility in regard to the racial problem. The low-income history of minorities has meant that they have been poorly served in the housing market, and to this misfortune has been added the cleverly administered indignities of exclusion and discrimination. The saving virtue of our society is that we can use a responsive government to offset and correct such derelictions of the private business system.

NOTES

1. Glenn H. Beyer, *Housing: A Factual Analysis* (New York, Macmillan, 1959).
2. We need only recall the sensational "Windfall" scandals of the 1950's that cost the Federal Government millions.
3. For information about the real estate field see A. M. Sakolski, *Land Tenure and Land Taxation* (New York, Schelkenbach Foundation, 1957) and P. J. Davies, *Real Estate in American History* (Washington, D.C., Public Affairs Press, 1958).
4. See Statements by Commissioner, the Reverend Theodore Hesburgh, *Hearings of the U. S. Civil Rights Commission, 1960* (Washington, D.C., U. S. Government Printing Office, 1960), p. 508.
5. McEntire, *Residence and Race*, p. 219.
6. *Ibid.*, p. 225.
7. *Ibid.*, p. 267.
8. Negroes have paid handsomely in interest on conventional loans for this privilege. See *Hearings of the U. S. Civil Rights Commission, 1960*, p. 205, no. 12.
9. Abrams, *Forbidden Neighbors*, ch. vii.

10. *Ibid.*, ch. xx.
11. G. and E. Grier, *Discrimination in Housing* (New York, Anti-Defamation League, 1960), p. 35.
12. Handlin, *The Newcomers*, ch. iii.
13. Glazer and McEntire, *Studies in Housing and Minority Groups*, p. 4.
14. The editorials of *House and Home* on racial issues reflect this mentality. See quote by builder Roland Catarinella in *House and Home*, January 1959.
15. *Hearings of the U. S. Civil Rights Commission, 1960*, p. 485. 485.
16. Council for Civic Unity, San Francisco, *San Francisco's Housing Market—Open or Closed* (1960), p. 22.
17. For an account of how a real estate salesman was dismissed for selling to Negroes, see *Hearings of the U. S. Civil Rights Commission, 1960*, p. 484.
18. *San Francisco's Housing Market*, p. 17.
19. *Ibid.*, p. 16.
20. Sworn testimony before the Philadelphia Commission on Human Relations, Jeter vs. Byrne, October 10, 1960.
21. *Hearings of the U. S. Civil Rights Commission, 1960*, p. 712.
22. *Trends*; Bulletin of the National Committee against Discrimination in Housing, March-April, 1960.
23. See *Interracial Review*, June 1959.
24. See Sol Rabkin and Arnold Forster, "The Constitutionality of Laws Against Discrimination," *New York Law Forum*, January 1960.
25. See Chester Rapkin and William G. Grigsby, *The Demand for Housing in Racially Mixed Areas* (Berkeley, University of California Press, 1960), p. 2; and McEntire, *Residence and Race*, p. 169. For income data see E. J. Hughes, "The Negro's New Economic Life," *Fortune*, September 1956; and The National Urban League, *The Economic and Social Status of the Negro in the United States* (1961).
26. G. and E. Grier, *Privately Developed Interracial Housing* (Berkeley and Los Angeles, University of California Press, 1960).
27. See *Trends*; Bulletin of the National Committee against Discrimination in Housing, August-September, 1958.
28. Abrams, *Forbidden Neighbors*, p. 229.
29. Report of U. S. Civil Rights Commission, 1959.

5

Distant Neighbors

ONE OF THE most notable factors affecting the movement of Negroes and other people of color in the urban centers has, as we have seen, been the persistence of residential belts and islands of ethnic groups in the older neighborhoods. These concentrated ethnic groups have greatly influenced opinion and expectations about minorities. Historically, the immigrant foreign-language groups established the American form of the ghetto pattern in the large cities. Their segregation was partly forced but partly voluntary, permitting exit for those who were amenable to assimilation with the general population. These ethnic enclaves, with their traditionally inferior living conditions, were the matrix for later and larger Negro segregation areas.

When the great Negro migration to the cities began around World War I, the ethnic groups were a very considerable portion of the urban population. In 1920 the foreign-born represented 13% of our population.[1] As late as 1950 the central cities had very considerable percentages of foreign-born population. The foreign-born in some of the major cities and the non-white populations with which they were in juxtaposition are shown in the following table:*

* From *The Population of the United States* by Donald J. Bogue (Glencoe, Illinois, The Free Press, 1959), p. 147.

	Foreign Born	Non-White
New York	22%	9.8%
Chicago	14.5%	13.6%
Los Angeles	12.5%	8.7%
Philadelphia	11.2%	18.2%
Detroit	14.9%	16.2%
Boston	17.9%	4.1%

The proximity of non-whites and the foreign-born, when it did not yield an uneasy tolerance, produced confused resentment and hostility. The happy Fourth of July picture of hearty co-citizenship among all groups is misleading. While a practical tolerance usually functions, the attitudes and opinions underlying it are crude and well laced with antagonism. Although many immigrants have relaxed racial feelings, others have for years replenished the ranks of the race-conscious.

Immigrants from the Old World were no doubt tutored in the fine points of racial distinction by the native Americans.[2] Those with foreign-born ties were usually no less susceptible to prejudice and racial antagonism than the native-born citizens of long standing. Their concentration in ethnic pockets gave ample social expression to their willingness to reject intrusion and adhere to group loyalties. These groups became key factors in shaping the course of Negro movement through urban residential areas. In many places they rebuffed non-white entry into their areas or deflected it to other neighborhoods. At times they formed walls of resistance to non-white movement, or became swift evaders of non-white infiltration by moving away in concerted and disciplined fashion. The ethnic communities of the large cities have constituted an obstacle course through which the non-whites have had to move, now displacing, now surrounding, now outflanking the immigrant islands and foreign-language concentrations.

Obstacle Course

The primary consideration of the relationship of foreign-language communities to non-white population is that the "immigrant" neighborhoods have usually been physically contiguous or in apposition to non-white concentrations. The Negro and the foreign-language immigrant shared the limitations of income that forced them both to accept the older housing in the areas close to the center of the city. For the Negro this condition was more enduring. He remained confined, often while a succession of foreign-born groups came and went through the old neighborhoods. This physical proximity is important. It meant that the two types of minority groups, racial and lingual, were often in competition for the same shabby tenements and back-street houses. The foreign-born groups were often accustomed from their European background to working within circumscribed physical conditions. Their diligence and ingenuity would be lavished upon tiny areas that, however poor they seemed by general American standards, still represented relative comfort and security for the immigrant. As the foreign-born groups thinned out, they tended to shrink their concentrations or yield territory to others. Growing Negro population often filled the abandoned Irish, Italian or Slavic areas. But in order for the Negro to gain access to the general channels of urban movement, he frequently had to overcome or somehow bypass a tradition-rooted core of immigrant residence. These immigrant communities served as barriers against Negro mobility for the rest of the city population.

Examples of such roadblocks to Negro movements could be seen in St. Louis around 1930, where Germans, Jews, Poles and Italians bordered the Negro district west of the Mississippi.[3] "The Polish Principality" of Hamtramck in Detroit has for years been impenetrable by Negroes.[4] The ethnic ghettos along Franklin Street in North Philadelphia have long prevented the eastward movement of Negroes.[5]

The physical confrontation of the Negro and the white minority groups has been fraught with social factors that bedevilled the relationship. The foreign-born were often not sure of themselves at all in their new urban environment. Many were unused to democracy and its concepts of social and racial equality. Upon achieving some status in this new country, they felt they could not afford to have it undermined by mixing with the stigmatized non-white group. Although at times sensitive to discrimination themselves, they were in too precarious a social position to let this permit a softening in their own attitude toward the non-whites. The foreign-born groups were beset with many internal conflicts, and it was an easy response to direct hostility against the non-whites. The social conflicts and tensions accompanying the process of adjustment of the foreign-born to urban life tended to produce crime and delinquency, which sometimes became a behavior pattern within the groups. This turbulence became exceedingly dangerous when racial incidents took place.

To the tightly knit foreign-born groups the Negro was often a strange and dreadful creature. They would have less knowledge of him than even the native white American. He would not be another European like the rest of the minorities. He would not have the elaborate rituals and customs of the Europeans, but would seem to defy any cultural definition. As a competitor for jobs, space and facilities, he was a threat.

It is evident, then, that among the group antagonisms in American cities, the relationship between the Negro and the foreign-born presented special difficulties. "But this is all in the past. It was acted out in the early part of the century," some would say. This is too facile a judgment. The foreign-born communities have been tenacious. Some have thrived for generations.[6] In addition to the foreign-born persons in these groups, the second- and third-generation offspring are often strongly identified with ethnic ties.

Even where they have lost numbers and vitality, immigrant areas have imparted an identity to a section of the city. This identity is significant. People are often more impressed by reputations than by realities. Negroes may shun an area for a long while because of the area's reputation for hostility, despite opportunities to enter it.

In the 1960 Presidential election, ethnic groups in the large cities were still significant enough for politicians to attribute the course of the election to their voting.[7] The politics of the "balanced" ethnic ticket were still strong. The foreign-born communities were vocal and active in the 1950's. Their physical locales clearly remained. These groups, because they were distinctive and identifiable, could "set the tone" for an area where the actual group members were themselves a minority in a heterogeneous residential population. Although the days of foreign immigrant power and prominence in the large cities are on the wane, a great percentage of our population still thinks in terms of ethnic experience and concentrations that were traditional for decades in the urban centers. There even seems to be evidence of what could be called "echo ghettos," second- and third- and fourth-generation residence areas where there is a moderate, somewhat diffuse, but quite real ethnic affinity. Some suburban areas, for instance, may be populated rather heavily through a builder who has strong ties with an ethnic group and its old city neighborhood. Jews and Italians have certainly removed to new housing areas in various places with a high degree of cohesiveness.[8]

Samuel Lubell has written: "The frustrations of the urban frontier, however, fall most heavily on the older residential areas, along the line where expanding Negro settlement pushes in on those unable to rise higher on the social ladder. Along this racial 'middle border,' where the rainfall of social status is so uncertain, the emotions stirred by the civil rights issue assume their most violent form. Most of the anti-Negro incidents of recent years have occurred in this zone of new Negro residential penetration."[9]

Within the neighborhoods where life is so animated and flavored by the languages, customs and mentalities of the foreign-born there are social ferments and cults that take on a special virulence in the immigrant environment. These currents of behavior and thinking may even become part of the self-image of the ethnic group, responses to be expected on the urban scene. Thus the working-class pugnacity of a Polish neighborhood has an especially formidable quality. The teen-age gangs of Italian neighborhoods, often aping the adult racketeer elements so long associated with Italian lower-status areas, represent a sort of urban tradition of renegade behavior because they have become so familiar. The "lace curtain" status nerves of bourgeois Irish families are highly vulnerable to racial change. These dynamics of immigrant group life form part of the interaction between the races in urban areas. Each group has it own dispositions and expressions of juvenile hostility, group resentment and status fears.

It is not possible in a book of this size to provide an exhaustive examination of the bearing of ethnic concentration of various kinds on non-white movements. It is possible to present illustrative considerations of certain foreign-language or ethnic groups and their relationships to nearby Negro concentrations. The information that follows should be in no way construed as indicative of any thoroughgoing social malady in the groups discussed. These groups all have remarkable qualities and have made remarkable contributions to American life. Their difficulties with the racial question, though more severe or more immediate because of their physical proximity to Negro-occupied areas, are part of the more general vexation of our society on this issue. We will look, then, at some of the groups whose position in the urban demographic pattern exposes them to the test of tolerance on race relations.

The Poles. People with race relations experience contend that Polish neighborhoods are particularly resistant to racial change and are likely to react violently to incursions by non-whites. Areas of Polish immigrant or other Slavic concentration have been the scenes of some of the most notable outbursts of racial violence in Northern cities. Violence in Detroit is often ascribed to Polish elements, as were outbreaks in Cicero, Illinois, adjacent to Chicago.[10]

The Poles are noted as a highly individualistic people, a people caught in historic contradictions. The history of the mother country may be very significant in explaining the Polish attitude toward group relationships in this country. Poland's shifting borders and political life have embraced a number of traditionally hostile ethnic and nationality groups. Within Poland there have been in modern times a variety of populations coexisting in uneasy polity. Lithuanians, Estonians, German-speaking elements, Ukrainians, White Russians, Jews and various Balkan strains have lived in Polish territory intermittently. The Poles have had a difficult time, to look at it from their viewpoint, with a long historical succession of fiery, separatist, unyielding, foreign-language and ethnic minorities. This accounts for some of the furious quality of Polish nationalism. With such a legacy of intergroup difficulty, it is not surprising that Poles did not come to the polyglot American city with a bland attitude toward minority neighbors in the New World.[11]

In the great monument of research on the Poles, *The Polish Peasant in Europe and America,* Thomas and Znaniecki point out a distinctive feature of Polish immigrant life.[12] They note that the Poles formed their mutual aid societies and social and fraternal groups before they concentrated residentially. This is important. It means that there was an especially deliberate character to Polish residential concentration. It did not take place in such a random fashion as that of other groups. While it was, no doubt, subject to the general exigencies of immigrant settlement, there was more consultation, direction and group influence in the choices that formed the Polish communities. Thus, the Polish neighborhood is less of an accident and more of a group bastion than the neighborhoods of most other immigrants.

Moreover, Polish families usually devote a great deal of energy and thrift to the care of dwellings. The house is a family project and all share in its improvement. In such areas as Detroit's Hamtramck, which has stood as an all-white area adjacent to Negro concentrations for years, the steady improvement of the housing is a tribute to the hard work of immigrant families. The reaction of such families to the encroachment of Negroes, whose residential history has been one of privation, is strongly resentful. The rough caliber of this resentment is described by one commentator on big city life. "The Poles, who for the most part live in neighborhoods that have not yet been entered by Negro families, are said to be determined to resist, with violence if necessary, any Negro invasion of the areas they inhabit. Political committeemen in Polish neighborhoods have vocally associated themselves with this attitude." [13]

As a minority group the Poles have not fared as well in the American immigrant sweepstakes as others. Bogue points that the second-generation Poles in the United States have actually a lower socio-economic status than the first generation.[14] Poles have also remained in a position near the bottom of the "social distance scale," a device drawn up by social scientists to reflect prevalent ethnic preferences.[15]

In terms of educational attainment, the Poles rank low among immigrant groups in this country.[16] The Jews and Irish do well in increasing the level of school years completed between first and second generation. Italians and others complete fewer years in school. These factors would certainly have an influence upon the race relations of the group. Deprivation of social status would heighten the likelihood that Poles would feel a need for a scapegoat. The Negro would be present, and often in a position to compete with the Pole for jobs and other opportunities. The lower educational achievement of the Pole would increase the possibility of unthinking and pugnacious responses to racial change.

Because the percentage of Polish-born persons in the population will decrease rapidly in coming years, and because residential mobility will continue to erode the old Polish-occupied neighborhoods, the acuteness of the racial problem with respect to this group is likely to diminish. Since the Poles are a predominantly Roman Catholic group, the gradual but pervasive Catholic moral concern for the elimination of racial inequities will have an effect as the educational level of people of Polish background rises.

The Italians.   Of all immigrant groups the Italians are most symbolic for the twentieth century of the great American experience of immigration. Of the major immigration groups, they were the last great wave to arrive from Europe in the tens of thousands. Their arrival was the denouement of the tremendous Atlantic migration. They seemed to enact the drama of building an urban ethnic world in American cities with a zestful enthusiasm. Numerically, the Italian-born are our largest foreign-born group. Their concentrations in the "Little Italys"

in the various cities are still very much with us. The Italian
neighborhoods are some of our most striking examples of ethnic
aggregation today, if we omit Negro neighborhoods from consideration.[17]

The Italian neighborhoods with their accompanying churches,
fraternal lodges, Italian food shops and gregarious family life
have not been confined to older large-city areas. Many smaller
industrial towns in the East, fruit-growing areas on the West
Coast and food-processing centers have strong Italian communities. We are most concerned, however, with the Italian-occu-
pied areas adjoining Negro districts. These older neighborhoods usually derived their Italian character from the first
waves of immigration from Southern Italy. Beginning in the
1880's and reaching its height in the early years of this century,
the tide ebbed after World War I. The exhaustion of the Sicilian
sulphur mines, the demise of feudal estates with political
change, the great disaster of the blight of the grapevines, and
the hope for a better life in America brought tens of thousands
of Italians to our urban areas. At times, the immigrants were
recruited for American industry by agents in Italy. Employment was found in railroad construction, the garment trades,
the building trades and food industries.

With some assurance of steady income the Italian immigrant
turned, characteristically, to the domestic world, the family
sphere focused on the neighborhood. He found himself in
second-rate residential areas or outright slums. The cohesiveness and energy of the Italian families was turned to making
these areas tolerable. The immigrant families seemed incur-
ably horticultural. Gardens were ingeniously worked into back-
yards, onto balconies and rooftops. The houses were colorfully
refurbished with a kind of casual Italian grace and flair. It is
true that these improvements were often only a cosmetic treatment of basically inadequate neighborhoods, but the neighbor-

hoods became familiar, distinctive and alive. The vitality of
the large Italian families was imparted to the neighborhoods in
an informal but effective way. The Italian populations found
their leaders in civic and political life and developed a morale
and a distinct style of life which impregnated the local area.

One striking feature of the Italian residential blocks has
been the housing improvements that have taken place under
private initiative. The extensive engagement of Italians in building trades meant that the families usually had valuable skills
available. The men could cut stone, lay brick and cement and
do a great number of things by way of physical improvement
of homes and shops. And, significantly, they could do these
things themselves well enough to be proud of the results. Owing
to the association of Negroes with shabby and deteriorated
houses, the financial and emotional investment of the Italian
householder was felt to be in jeopardy when Negroes en-
croached.

Also the Italian neighborhood has been steadily replenished
by second- and third-generation offspring. Strong family ties
induce a number of the younger families to stay within walking distance of parents and grandparents. The beloved "nona,"
the winemaking grandfather, the generous uncle or godparent
are just too well-accepted and compatible to desert.

Large families in small houses mean that the young will
seek the outdoors. In cities this means the street corner or some
familiar sandwich shop. In the Italian neighborhoods the
"pizza" shops and the soda fountain hangouts are the scenes
for second- and third-generation street-corner society. It is in
the relations of juvenile groups that antagonism between Negroes and white immigrant groups often flares up. The case of
Italian youths will be cited here, not because it is peculiar to
them, but because there are good examples of friction in Italian
neighborhoods in the case files of interracial and intergroup

relations agencies. A further complication to the racial issue may be a Latin concept of personal honor which requires an injury to be avenged. This would increase the possibility of hostile exchange.

In 1960 and early 1961, two cities provided examples of incidents involving Italians and Negroes. The incidents were largely independent of one another, but their combined impact on the respective Italian and Negro groups should be considered carefully because the outbreaks formed a clear sequence in popular opinion.

In Philadelphia in May 1960 a high school boy, John Campiglia, was killed by a "wolf pack" attack of Negro youths. The killing was utterly senseless and the victim utterly innocent. Public opinion in the Italian community was inflamed. A series of small fights and a retaliatory shotgun attack took place shortly afterward in the same section of the city. Fortunately, the shotgun blast only slightly injured a Negro girl on the steps of a Baptist Church. In June 1960 a young policeman named Marinelli was called to a melee in a heavily Negro area of North Philadelphia. He leaned from the door of his patrol wagon and fired his gun repeatedly at a fleeing man. He killed not only the man but a woman near him. Both victims were Negro. Both were innocent of any offense. Negro community opinion was outraged. In February 1961, while the trial of the killers of John Campiglia was in progress, the son of a civic leader in South Philadelphia named Ianelli was beaten by a teen-age gang of Negroes. The boy's father had been a worker for better race relations. In March 1961, a teen-ager named Cerone was stabbed by Negro boys after a basketball game (the wound resulting in paralysis). In the same month an emotionally disturbed Italian war-bride, wife of a Negro in an integrated community, attracted public notice by placing anti-Negro signs around her home and engaging in other anti-Negro activity. These incidents, with the publicity attending them, formed a pattern for the Italian and Negro groups. Their effect was to add fuel to smoldering hostility and to start a chain-reaction of aggravating incidents which heightened the possibility of a general outbreak.

In New York in a twelve-month period there were a series of Italian-Negro-Puerto Rican conflicts. In East Harlem, Negroes and Puerto Ricans began an attempt to enter an old Italian neighborhood. In Greenwich Village Negro passengers from Harlem caused resentment when detraining from the subway lines. In New York's oldest "Little Italy," around Canal and Mulberry Streets in lower Manhattan, a killing and a teen-age conflict involving Italians, Puerto Ricans and Negroes caused high tension. Serious intergroup conflicts occurred in the Cooper Park area of Williamsburg, where a low-income housing project with many Negro occupants was located in the midst of an Italian community. In the Park Slope area of Brooklyn, pitched battles in the streets between gangs armed with guns, tire irons and all the weapons of hoodlumism, occurred in a largely Italian neighborhood.[18] The fights occurred after Puerto Ricans had begun moving into the area and verbal insults were exchanged.

These incidents are typical of the violence that plagues the relationship between ethnic groups. The events are usually given sensationalized coverage in the general press as well as being reported in the Italian- and Spanish-language papers and the Negro press. People conscious of ethnic identity take sides, connecting the incidents with a special kind of rivalry. The chance of retaliation is increased by the proximity of the groups. Such series of events are common in the large cities. The hostility thus generated may come to a head at any time, to provide the tinder for large-scale racial violence. Fortunately, for blessed but obscure reasons, it seldom does.

The Jews.　Jewish people are wise in the ways of cities. They have for centuries been an urban people. Time after time they have seen racial antagonism mount in city streets. It is improbable, however, that they have ever encountered on such a large scale the kind of problem presented by the urbanization of the American Negro. The entire social life of the modern city is momentously different from that of the past. In the past, population movement was slow; today there is swift movement resulting in an almost random mixture of people from various backgrounds in metropolitan centers. In this setting the large Jewish populations of the major northern cities are involved in a very distinctive way in the nation's struggle to resolve the "American Dilemma" of race relations.[19]

One of the places in which Negroes confront Jews is the corner store. In many of the great segregated districts the last outposts of white residence are the groceries, small dry-goods stores and pharmacies which are in many cases owned and operated as family businesses by modestly prosperous Jewish people. Because of their economic stake in these small businesses, the owners have frequently been reluctant to leave areas which have changed racially. In segregated neighborhoods where the earning power and standard of living are often depressed, these little stores fit intimately into neighborhood life. They are flexible enough to meet the irregular needs of informal local and family living. In overcrowded Negro districts the street-corner society which affords an outlet to the young centers around such small businesses.

In these circumstances the Jewish storekeeper is often the only white man many Negroes see on a regular basis. He is a person who gives service, but often he is also a family creditor to whom the grocery bill is owed. The amount of anti-Semitism that may grow out of this latter relationship is surprising. As the last white resident on the block in sections where existence is less than genteel, it is understandable that the small shop-keeper should at times feel the pressure of minority-group frustration and counter-prejudice.

A second "sphere of influence" in which Negroes and Jews interact is in those heavily Jewish neighborhoods that have begun to change racially. The sequence of migrations of minority groups through our cities has often placed Negroes next in line to Jews in social status and home-buying ability. Neighborhoods once forbidden to Jews have received substantial influxes of Jewish home owners. Because of geographical convenience or economic accessibility, these same neighborhoods are now attractive to non-white home buyers. The aspiring Negro sees in these areas the same virtues of middle-class respectability that Jewish families, fresh from the immigrant "Jewtowns," saw in them a generation ago. Perhaps there is also some basis for supposing that the "liberal" opinion prominent in big-city Jewish circles and the traditionally non-violent disposition of Jews exert an attraction on Negroes seeking a way out of segregated neighborhoods.

In neighborhoods where Jews form a very substantial portion of the population there has been no marked deviation from the general pattern of response to Negro newcomers. Essentially the white reaction remains the same. The likelihood of violence is at a minimum, but the development of panic and gradual white withdrawal is the usual course.[20] Community leadership sympathetic toward racial integration does seem to be more frequent in such areas, but this does not change the eventual outcome. The promotion of interracial understanding still comes "too little and too late" to be of any practical significance.

There are other influences that seem to make neighborhoods with heavy Jewish populations susceptible to racial turnover. For many Jewish families, long in the urban tradition, the

processes of property exchange contain no mystery. They enter
without hesitation into real estate transactions when the question arises of leaving a changing neighborhood. In addition, in
a group keenly preoccupied with education, the coming of Negroes to the public school seems, in the light of racial stereotypes, like a blow to the educational advantages and prospects
of Jewish children. Other factors permitting greater mobility
are the small size of Jewish families and the relatively high proportion of Jews who live in apartments instead of owning
houses.[21] In any event, the middle-class status of the bulk of
the Jewish population usually assures some assets with which
to negotiate a property sale.

The problem of a synagogue in a racially changing area
should also be noted. Unlike many Christian denominations,
the Jews do not proselytize. The synagogue congregation can
not absorb incoming Negro families the way a correctly oriented Roman Catholic or a Congregational or Methodist
Church can, and reduction in the congregation due to the removal of a Jewish family is likely to be permanent. If a sufficient proportion of the congregation migrates, it may be
economically mandatory for the temple to follow. This is one
reason for the growth of the "echo ghetto" in the suburbs. The
old downtown congregation re-forms in the new area.

The third sphere in which Negroes and Jews are particularly
linked is not so much physical as it is one of social psychology.
The Negro and Jew are both members of a minority group
that experienced a sour tolerance or actual ill-treatment on
the American scene. This fact has brought forth a sort of kin-
ship or practical affinity between Jews and Negroes, based on
their common concern for fair treatment and democratic rights.
Hence Jewish and Negro organizations can usually be found
working together for civil rights, fair employment, intergroup
understanding and racial integration. Many Jewish groups de-

vote more effort to bettering race relations than to any other object.

Opposite these factors facilitating contact between Negroes and Jews must be ranged certain social characteristics of each group which serve to produce a distressing tension between them. Despite the strong affinity that we have noted, there is a great cultural difference between the Jew and Negro. This is not just a difference between a group long urbanized and one of very recent agrarian background. It is a difference of cultural heritage and experience. Although the Negro folk culture had as a cardinal element a familiarity with and reverence for the Bible, and notably for the prophets and kings of Israel, there is a vast difference between the Jewish view of this heritage and the Negro folk view of it. The complexity of the unique Jewish tradition, heavy with history, stands in strong contrast to the youth and the directness of the American Negro orientation. This contrast is made most vivid when we compare the educational status of the two groups. American Jews have from the time of their immigration achieved an extraordinary educational eminence. In terms of formal schooling, they enjoy a top position among American ethnic groups. Negroes, on the other hand, are still struggling under the educational disabilities inflicted upon them by segregation and exploitation. In education Negroes and Jews are further apart than any of the other groups in the mainstream of American life.

In family life and in the incidence of crime Jew and Negro are also in vivid contrast. The ceremonial of the Jewish home has no parallel in highly variable Negro domestic life. The widely publicized crimes of some Negroes which glare from the pages of metropolitan newspapers have a bewildering effect on many Jewish citizens, who seem unable to comprehend that such things can exist. The American Jew, largely middle-class in thought and demeanor, is out of touch with the world of rejection, privation and violence to which the Negro has been assigned by current social forces.

The American Jew shares actively in the economic abundance that has been the nation's harvest for the last fifteen years. He walks with non-Jews as leader, organization man and laborer in the economic activities of the day. He inhabits suburbia and plays a vigorous role both as producer and consumer. The Negro, by contrast, is just beginning to emerge from an economic limbo. His family income, job status, savings and property ownership are all below the national average for whites, and nobody really knows how much of the recent progress of Negroes in these areas has been achieved at the expense of such sacrifices as the employment of mothers and the postponement of medical and educational needs.

In social organization we perceive once again a great disparity between Jew and Negro. Jews have an enviable apparatus of fraternal, charitable, and civic organizations manned by articulate and effective leaders. Negroes are still suffering from the paucity of leadership that has been a traditional characteristic of depressed ethnic groups arriving on the urban scene. Men like Martin Luther King are exceptional in any group. The ability of a group to train and consistently present skilled leadership is slow-growing. Leadership in effective force does not rise out of a vacuum; it must have preconditions of education, organized tradition, a degree of leisure and concourse with the elites of power and learning.

In addition to these social contrasts between Negro and Jew there is the difference in the commitment each group bears to ideals of community life. Whatever our predictions about the future, we must recognize that at present Negroes do most emphatically exist as a social group. As such, they seem to have largely renounced the ideal of racial solidarity in favor of a ratherly loosely constructed racial affiliation permitting full integration, when possible, into the general community. In this respect non-whites seem to have a somewhat unreserved commitment to the undifferentiated "liberal" egalitarian community. Jews, on the other hand, have a distinctive ideal of community life with deep religious implications. This historic ideal, which antedates by ages the "open community" concept, is operative today in the voluntary residential clustering around synagogues which produces heavily Jewish neighborhoods in our big cities. These two community ideals, that of the religiously based community and that of the open community based upon secular citizenship, are not mutually exclusive, but they can lead to divergent views on questions of intermarriage, community life and education which are of mutual concern to both Jews and Negroes.

An examination of the relationship between the Negro and the Jew in the light of the social factors mentioned above indicates that there is a considerable social gap between the two groups in spite of the bond of sympathy they share. One of the practical effects of this situation is that Jews are often placed under extreme pressures when they face up to racial issues. Often Jewish people solidly supporting liberal race relations practices and programs feel genuinely repelled by the social differences persisting in the Negro population when racial integration confronts them, and they are brought face to face with the contrasts between the great bulk of the newly urbanized Negro population and their own established middle class. Thus Jews do seem to have a special problem with respect to racial change.

Puerto Ricans. Although Puerto Rican migration to the mainland has not brought about a great dispersion of Spanish-speaking people generally through the Eastern cities, it has resulted in strong Puerto-Rican concentrations in the old neighborhoods of Philadelphia, Chicago, Bridgeport and, above all,

New York. The influx has thus placed the Puerto Ricans in some of the major urban centers which are today vast laboratories of social tension and racial change. Placed beside American Negroes or intermingled with them, the Puerto Ricans have been very confused in their racial attitudes. Their Hispanic background has endowed them with a rather casual attitude toward race. This attitude is subtle. In the mainland cities, the keen consciousness of race among the general population forces Puerto Ricans to question their own tradition in racial matters, and frequently to adopt a more decisive attitude towards racial differences in response to the mainland aberrations.[22] But this is done with much inner confusion.

Racial distinctions in Puerto Rico are mild, but they are there. The Spanish terms of *el blanco* (white), *el indio* (dark skin with straight hair), *el grifo* (white coloring, but with hair or features of a negroid cast), *el bien triguena* (a fairer Negro) and the use of the term *el Negro* as a word of opprobrium reflect the differing values ascribed to racial visibility on the island. Within the Puerto Rican group, however, particularly in Puerto Rico, color is inconsequential in social relations. In families there will sometimes be a subtle feeling of status difference based on color between siblings, but this is seldom serious. On the mainland, this attitude of casual acceptance can suddenly become starkly challenged, and the emotional impact on family life and personal awareness can be tremendous.[23]

The acute in-group feeling and loyalty in the Puerto Rican communities induces the Hispanos to reject the American Negro on double grounds; first as an outsider, and second as a symbol of and a target for racial discrimination with which it would be unwise to be identified. The Spanish-speaking Puerto Rican of dark color is fraternally treated—except, perhaps, on the mainland where there is question of intimate or permanent relationships—but the American Negro is an interloper, a threat, a puzzle. The fact that similar disabilities afflict both groups in many ways only heightens the Puerto Rican's resentment against the American Negro. Thus Puerto Ricans may resent appeals against prejudice and discrimination which link American Negroes and Hispanos.[24]

Puerto Ricans in New York and elsewhere have been harbingers of racial change. In East Harlem, the Bronx and Brooklyn they have preceded Negro entries.[25] Having the Puerto Ricans in the role of precursors has not noticeably slowed the classic white response of withdrawal upon Negro influx. In the mainland cities, the relations between American Negroes and Puerto Ricans have commonly been strained, with juvenile fights the most frequent expression of this antagonism. The tension seems greatest with respect to newly arrived Puerto Ricans. There is some moderation of hostility as the groups reside in the same area over a period of time.[26] Small groups will become friends and establish ties casually in the second or third generation, but the barrier to intimate association will usually remain.

There is the old area competition between the two groups for jobs and housing. The Negro resents the arrival of the Puerto Rican to work for lower pay. Puerto Ricans who open small shops and stores accuse Negroes of being stupid or lazy because they have in the main been slow to build such businesses. Any advances made by Hispanos are subject to criticism by Negroes because the Puerto Rican, not born on the mainland and speaking a foreign language, is successful "at the expense of Negroes."[27]

While Hispanos and Negroes may resent one another, their residential association is constantly enforced. The Puerto Ricans are recently arrived in the cities, and so are many Southern Negroes. Landlords are seldom capable of according the groups separate status, although the language factor may make property rental more difficult for the Hispanos. The distinction and separation is made at the insistence of the Puerto Ricans, who tend to choose dwellings removed from Negro occupancy, so far as this is possible in areas crowded by the adjacent groups.

Perhaps the chief factor separating the two groups, besides the consciousness of color, is a difference in attitudes about sex and the family. At the neighborhood level this is extremely important, for the residential world is a domestic one. The Hispano family is extended, proud, and has a careful code of behavior and relationships prescribed by long tradition. The Negro family is nuclear, weakened by many long-term influences and informal in its relationships. In the Puerto Rican family, the male has high status. In the Negro family, the woman has so often been breadwinner that she is the main figure. Puerto Ricans resent the easy approach to women that mainland Negroes may exhibit. For Puerto Ricans the woman is guarded by a protective supervision of attitudes and customs. Hence there is a subtle strategy of withdrawal among the Spanish-speaking families which evades advances by American Negroes, even though life may be proceeding on a friendly basis. The Negro, who may have encountered promiscuous contacts between Puerto Rican males and American Negro women, sees no reason why the compliment shouldn't be returned by Puerto Rican women, especially since many may be just as dark as he is.

There are other divergences in churches and in recreation. Some commentators state that integration of the mainland Negroes and Puerto Ricans is far away.[28] The two groups will continue to share the worst of the housing supply, with the Puerto Rican frequently unable to escape identification with the Negro, although residential segregation of necessity will operate less precisely in the case of some Spanish-speaking because they are not readily identifiable as colored. The Puerto Rican will continue to be the "alter ego" of the mainland Negro in residential matters.

The Negro neighborhoods adjoining the white minority communities have an ambiguous set of attitudes toward their "distant neighbors." On the one hand, the immigrants are subject to some discrimination, as is the Negro. In some ways relationships may be casual and unprejudiced. Negroes may shop in the curbside Italian markets, or go to school with Puerto Ricans or realize that Jewish organizations are pro-integration. On the other hand, there will be a recognition that the immigrants do constitute a group by themselves, with their own exclusive clubs and programs, and the Negro will know that acquiring a house in the immigrant area will mean trouble.

For the Negro population the significance of the white immigrant as a member of a minority group tends to be obscured by the simple fact that the immigrant is white, thereby sharing the negative characteristics of the stereotyped white person so common in the thinking of Negroes. It is frequently observed by native Negroes, with some bitterness, that they are denied opportunities which the foreign-born can easily obtain. The resettlement of Hungarian refugees after the disorders in that country in 1956 aroused resentment in Negro circles. As they saw it, persons who had made no contribution to this country were fussed over by the government and resettled in good houses in good neighborhoods. Negroes couldn't occupy those same houses without bringing the scorching wrath of their fellow citizens down on their heads.

On succeeding some immigrant population in an area, Negroes often find that the housing is owned by a number of absentee landlords of the previous immigrant group. The Negro families may face rent gouging and other forms of exploitation, and their attitude toward the group represented by the landlords may become hostile. The activities of immigrant savings and loan societies which control property or immigrant fraternal groups who purchase property to keep it out of the hands of Negroes produce the same kind of negative reaction.

The Muslim and Black Nationalist groups which have been widely publicized in recent years are not averse to singling out Jews and other groups for special indictment in race relations. These Negro extremist cults do not represent any large segment of Negro opinion, but their arguments in this matter will usually be listened to with care by a great number of Negroes, who may be familiar with the racial thinking of white ethnic groups.

As the inquirer proceeds to the more educated levels of Negro life, however, he finds that the commitment of Negroes to tolerance and interracial fellowship offsets bad experiences. The informed and intelligent Negro seldom singles out particular white ethnic groups for criticism in racial matters, but tends to argue in terms of the white population as a whole.

Native Whites. Although we have concentrated our attention upon foreign-born groups in this chapter, it should not be inferred that cohesive, native-born neighborhoods are not a frequent source of trouble. The problems arising from neighborhoods with a high percentage of Appalachian mountaineers have been of considerable concern in some cities. Cities with a high home-ownership rate, where neighborhoods are stable and the population relatively settled, produce the phenomenon of entrenched "burghers," with practically no immigrant ties, who yet vigorously oppose racial change. Such areas are not nearly so troublesome as immigrant locales, but they indicate that it is not so much immigrant peculiarities as the fundamental sense of group cohesion which threatens social harmony in racial situations.

The population elements deriving from "the old immigration" of the early nineteenth century have, of course, been

deeply enmeshed in the traditions of racial exclusion and restriction. Whatever our estimate of the reactions of new immigrant groups, we must not forget that these groups have been
entering into an American stream of social opinion in which
racism was a strong current. The upper-class and middle-class
neighborhoods of the successful "old immigration" elements
were the models for the newer arrivals.

There are forces at work in native-born neighborhoods that
on occasion can produce agitated waves of racial feeling, although such areas seldom hold the same violence potential as
immigrant communities. The insecurity of the "junior executive" suburb is an example. In a suburb of "organization man"
families, the corporations that control the jobs of the breadwin-
ners may transfer a household head to another city on short
notice. Hence the home owners are extremely sensitive to anything which would make the selling of their houses more difficult. The presence of Negroes in the area is such a factor. This
"junior executive" difficulty was thought to be one of the reasons why the suburban town of Deerfield, Illinois, reacted with
hostility to a plan to erect a limited number of attractive homes
for interracial occupancy nearby.

Another reaction in native-born "old immigration" areas in
recent years has been the product of a decline into minority
status on the part of formerly predominant groups. Old-line
white Protestant communities in large cities, where the populations are increasingly Catholic and Negro, are beginning to
display all the marks of minority psychology. They feel hemmed
in, discriminated against, objects of the ill-will of the growing
Negro and Catholic elements. Security and self-possessed assurance are beginning to wane under the impact of metropolitan population mobility and changes in the urban power structure. Even though many of the old-line neighborhoods and
suburbs are not yet confronted with racial change, they have
had to admit Jews, Italians and a variety of other formerly

proscribed groups. Having been nudged this far, the old-line residents have begun to fear that the next step, racial change, is inevitable. This is a reaction that is not found among the hardier new immigrants, who are often ready to contest each street in their area.

The shifting population of the urban centers will alter the residential make-up in the central city areas. Only vestiges of the immigrant communities will remain. For some years yet, however, these communities will have a special significance for race relations. In most of the larger cities the municipal intergroup relations agencies have representation from the different ethnic groups on their boards or in staffs. This at least permits some communication with the groups so that when conflict situations or severe tensions arise, there can be consultation and the exertion of accepted leadership to avoid outbreaks or the continuation of hostility. Formal representation of ethnic groups on those civic bodies committed to peace and fair play increases the possibility that mutual respect will be maintained. The leadership of each group is loath to be stigmatized as irresponsible or incendiary in the eyes of the other group. Such a formula for civic peace in the diversified urban community can be effective if it is well administered and serviced with an adequate program of information, conference and involvement of representative opinion leaders. But if the formula is mere window-dressing, a coalition of ethnic leaders for mutual admiration and ego-gratification or for the sake of political display, then the city that permits such a fraud may find its peace broken and its minority group relations poisoned by antagonism.

The day of immigrant neighborhoods may be fading fast, but these areas have had a strategic significance in the last two decades in their effect upon non-white urban movement. They represent a notable interlude in intergroup relations. The lessons we can learn from them should not be readily forgotten.

NOTES

1. Donald J. Bogue, *The Population of the United States* (Glencoe, Ill., The Free Press, 1959), p. 124.

2. In its early years the Ford Motor Company has been reported to have fostered inter-ethnic rivalry and prejudice to forestall union organization. See L. P. Smith, *The Torch of Liberty* (New York, Dwight-King Co., 1959), p. 31.

3. Queen and Carpenter, *The American City*, p. 135. For a general study of the ethnic history of a city see Handlin, *The Newcomers*.

4. Abrams, *Forbidden Neighbors*, ch. ix.

5. Philadelphia Commission on Human Relations, *Non-White Residential Patterns* (1959).

6. See Walter Firey, *Land Use in Central Boston* (Cambridge, Harvard University Press, 1947), for a documentation of the Italian community in Boston.

7. "G.O.P. Loss Is Laid to Big Cities," *New York Times*, Sunday, February 26, 1961.

8. See Federation of Jewish Agencies of Greater Philadelphia, *Analysis of Movement of Jewish Families* (1958).

9. Lubell, *The Future of American Politics*, p. 90.

10. See Abrams, *Forbidden Neighbors*, p. 95; and Allen Grimshaw, "A Study of Social Violence—Urban Race Riots in the United States," an unpublished doctoral dissertation, University of Pennsylvania, 1959.

11. Drake and Cayton, *The Black Metropolis*, cites prejudice among Poles (pp. 181-182).

12. Queen and Carpenter, *The American City*, cites this data on page 137.

13. James Reichley, *The Art of Government: Reform and Organization Politics in Philadelphia*, a report to the Fund for the Republic, 1960, pp. 79-80.

14. Bogue, *The Population of the United States*, p. 374. See also E. P. Hutchinson, *Immigrants and Their Children* (New York, Wiley, 1956).

15. Emory Bogardus, *Immigration and Race Attitudes* (New York, Heath, 1928).

16. Bogue, *The Population of the United States,* p. 368.

17. The persistence of Italian concentration is examined by Walter Firey in *Land Use in Central Boston.*

18. "Terror Stalks Slope in Wake of Race Riot," *New York Daily News,* February 23, 1961.

19. Material similar to the remarks here recorded appeared in Dennis Clark, "Urban Negro and Urban Jew," *The Crisis,* May 1958.

20. Louis Wirth years ago noted the peaceful reception Negroes got in Jewish areas. Cf. "Racial Segregation in the City," *American Journal of Sociology,* July 1927.

21. The Editors of Fortune Magazine, *The Exploding Metropolis,* p. 195.

22. One author, for instance, cites the fact that Puerto Ricans are told by police in some places to stay away from Negroes. See Clarence Senior, *Strangers, Then Neighbors* (New York, Anti-Defamation League of B'nai B'rith, 1961), p. 27. There is evidence that Puerto Ricans also become subject to conflicts with other immigrant groups. See Robert O'Brien, *A Survey of Puerto Ricans in Lorain, Ohio* (Delaware, Ohio, Wesleyan University Press, 1954).

23. See Dan Wakefield, *Island in the City* (Boston, Houghton, 1959), pp. 40-41.

24. See Elena Padilla *Up from Puerto Rico* (New York, Columbia University Press, 1958), p. 53.

25. Wakefield, *op. cit.,* p. 41.

26. Padilla, *op. cit.,* p. 93.

27. Christopher Rand, *The Puerto Ricans* (New York, Oxford, 1958), p. 131.

28. See, for instance, "Minister Sees Lag on Puerto Ricans," *The New York Times,* March 6, 1961.

6

Streets of Danger

MANY TIMES Negroes have learned that the streets of white neighborhoods are for them streets of danger. The passions aroused by racial resentment have often come to a climax in violence and vandalism. Negroes who penetrated all-white residential areas have all too frequently run a gauntlet of harassments and assault and lived in a state of siege. Violence aimed at discouraging Negroes from occupying property is a cruel factor in retarding mobility in the urban centers. Houses that are accessible to the Negro economically and may be only a short walk from depressed Negro areas are thus put beyond the reach of qualified minority families.

A little violence goes a long way. Most people count on avoiding trouble and conflict, and anyone who has once experienced violence personally or even seen it remembers it. Since ours is a generally peaceful society, with physical clashes rare except at the lowest social levels, they make a vivid impression when they do occur. In a person familiar with assaults against a group of which he is a member, apprehension is a fact of life. People who seek out danger and difficulty are rare. Violence in civil life has a special resonance, and racial violence is so bizarre, so dangerous in its implications, that the fear of it is almost instinctive.

There have been some studies of violence in race relations.[1] These have usually dealt with the worst kinds of explosion, those general outbreaks of fighting and property damage that are classified as full-scale race riots. Studies of lynching have been made by both historians and social psychologists.[2] One of the best single works concerning racial violence is probably the unpublished doctoral thesis "A Study in Social Violence— Urban Race Riots in the United States," by Alan Grimshaw, which not only documents incidents and presents extensive bibliography but tries to probe deeply into the social dynamics of urban racial conflicts.[3] Even this scholarly work omits an evaluation of the extent to which violence affects the movement of minority population in the urban housing market. Such a study is indeed a considerable undertaking, involving as it does economics and personal and social psychology. We shall in this chapter attempt to gain some estimate of the relation of violence to minority housing choices.

Why Violence?

In many urban neighborhoods violence is the ultimate argument in race relations. When emotion has reached a certain pitch and all alternative methods of checking the advance of the minority group have failed, violence becomes the last resort in the mind of the racist citizen. The use of physical force to rebuff or repel minority families has a great impact. Directed at a family, it is more frightening than that which a single minority group member might encounter in the course of his employment, recreation or transportation. This is so because an attack on the home touches intimately and profoundly the fundamental emotional springs of family life.

From the point of view of the white residents this violence involves high stakes. To the responsible elements in civic life it means that community peace and order are threatened—a rare thing in a country where the rule of law is accepted. It also means that the sacred totem of the middle and upper classes, property, is threatened. The possibility that violence might come helps to reinforce the conservatism of community leadership and the status quo in race relations and population distribution.

To the great mass of the prejudiced, violence is a confirmation of all their worst fears about the evils which Negroes or other minorities bring with them. These people see their property values threatened, believing that racial change automatically depresses prices. Since their houses are the greatest single investments of their lives, it is little wonder that some will resort to violence in a misguided attempt to "protect" themselves. When to the consideration of property is added the fact that the white resident sees his whole way of life challenged by non-white entry into the neighborhood, the intensity of feeling can hardly be imagined. To the white home owner, it is not only property, but sanitation, health, order, chastity, prestige and educational values that are threatened by racial change.

The Victims

To the Negro or other minority family which is the target of racial violence, the assault is deeply significant if it is related to housing.[4] The whole family is involved. It is not only a man's choice to bear the hostility and peril; the man's wife and children must share it. It is one thing for an adult male to brave difficulties, but to commit his family, in all its innocence and defenselessness, to the hazards of full-time residence in a sharply hostile environment is more than most family heads can bear. Perhaps a man might be confident that his wife could stand the tension and worry of guarded and alert living during a period of initial hostility, but it would be a rare father who could insert his children into such a situation without severe misgivings.

For the Negro family moving into a hostile white neighborhood there is tremendous strain. The parent who took the lead in choosing the house may feel the strain disproportionately. The housewife is in all likelihood home alone most of the day and may be alone some evenings if her husband works long hours or goes to evening school. "Housewife's loneliness" can be wearing enough without the threat of attack hanging over the household. The children must make their way to school, where perhaps they will be harassed in the schoolyard if they are small, or, if they are teen-agers, threatened by gangs. It is not easy for intelligent people to think of their children suffering taunts or other abuse, especially since the person imagining these things from a distance usually tends to exaggerate them. For the father of the beleaguered Negro family, his daily absence at work may be an agonizing ordeal. He must feel keenly the vulnerability of his relatively isolated family, and yet he is powerless to protect them, since the aggression is for the most part chiefly a psychological phenomenon, with actual physical challenge unpredictable.[5]

The house of the Negro family will soon become commonly identified if there has been considerable concern over the new arrival. It will become the focus of attention in many cases. Because it is a house, it will be immovable, a standing symbol of racial change, a stationary target. Thus, acts of violence against the property or its occupants are likely to be calculated, not like those flare-ups resulting from racial friction which occur at transportation points, amusement areas or in accidental encounters. There may be a long campaign of malicious harassments, including repeated damages to the property, productive of a perpetual war of nerves.[6] This is a hard situation to face, no matter how badly your family needs or wants a better house.

Because an urban neighborhood is usually rather shocked by violence, it is common for the residents to blame it on outsiders, ignoring the fact that local attitudes are solidly opposed to Negro entry and that local residents have far greater opportunities to commit the acts of vandalism. But the likelihood that the aggressions can be recurrent and wholly unpredictable because of the round-the-clock proximity of the antagonists is one of the most fearful thoughts that the Negro family must face.

Urban neighborhoods are densely populated and contain within them people of many social backgrounds. In a modest middle-class area there may be severely disturbed persons with histories of mental illness. Some neighbors with long careers of violence in military service may speak blandly of gasoline bombs and firearms. Still others may have lived for years in social situations where physical assault was cheerfully accepted as regular recreational activity.[7] These incalculable human factors added to an environment of intense racial feeling would be enough to produce acute anxiety in a phlegmatic person without family responsibilities. How much greater is the effect on a responsible family head beset by the problems of moving his household effects and altering his domestic routines? It is little wonder that Negroes have been reluctant to cross traditional racial boundary lines.

Combat Conditions

The conditions that dispose a residential area toward violence are worth examining. There are factors other than the
simple process of racial change that evoke violent reactions.
Grimshaw states that "in many areas, changing neighborhood
patterns, even in the absence of strong police control, have not
increased social tensions to the point where social violence has
occurred."[8] While many areas have changed peacefully, what
violence there has been has had its locus in the racially "contested" area. Thus, the same author says, "Except for the peak
period of major race riots, contested areas have been the location of most social racial violence in Northern urban areas."[9]
Grimshaw found several elements consistently present in various situations where racial violence erupted. These elements
can be listed here, and other local influences can be included in
an enumeration which relates the violence-producing conditions to the specific considerations surrounding housing purchases and rentals.

The challenge of accepted racial patterns is one condition
that usually precedes violence. The unwritten law that bars
Negroes from residing in this or that area is ordinarily challenged by actual occupancy of a property, but simply the appearance of a Negro has been construed as a challenge in some
cases.[10] A prospective buyer visiting a house is an obvious challenge, but even a Negro salesman or a colored person lost and
asking directions is enough to arouse resentment in some neighborhoods.

Grimshaw and others have also found that if the period of
rising tension has been protracted, violence is more likely. This
is an important factor in housing cases, because word of the
sale or rental of a house can leak out long before the Negro

occupants actually arrive. In cases where selling to Negroes is an act of spite or retaliation, the seller may let the fact be known. Almost all sales require negotiations and settlement arrangements which delay occupancy of a property. A thirty-day or sixty-day delay of this sort may be unavoidable, but it does have the unfortunate effect of permitting neighborhood opinion to crystallize. The mystery of who will occupy the property in question becomes a big local issue. During the waiting period anxiety may be fed by rumors, or visits to the property by workmen or agents. The tension tends to mount as speculation increases. The waiting period prior to occupancy is thus a key element in the exacerbation of local opinion which may lead to outbursts of unruly behavior.

The consciousness of racial matters and of bizarre events involving Negroes can be an important cause contributing to eventual violence at the neighborhood level. If Negroes have previously tried to enter an area and have been involved in notable difficulties, this can have a strong influence. And, as we pointed out earlier, events in Africa or Little Rock, crime stories involving Negroes in the press and other notoriety can heighten the tension. In many situations the mass media play a critical role with respect to such opinion. The sensationalizing of crime stories, the television or radio coverage of crowd situations, can mean the difference between informed opinion and inflamed opinion in racial matters. There is one case on record where prompt television coverage actually brought hundreds of curious viewers to the scene of the disturbance within minutes of the telecast.[11] Whether it is the grapevine of local gossip, the mass media or some extreme statement by a local leader, the heightening of the consciousness of race, added to the mores that support segregation, increases the possibility of violence and racial assaults.

Crime stories in which Negro lawbreakers are featured focus attention upon racial matters. News stories about rapes, muggings and "wolf-pack" attacks by gangs of Negro teen-agers do more than arouse resentment. They activate all the stereotypes of dark criminality that are part of the anti-Negro tradition. Such events, to the prejudiced mind, are clear evidence that the Negro has escaped control and now threatens urban safety and order. Paradoxically, this mentality sees retaliation or "revenge" police tactics as restorative of order. This kind of thinking forms the basis for violent rejection of Negro residential movement.

Intervention by professional racist agitators or by political subversives has not been a significant factor in residential violence in the North. In the South there has been ample aggression by native extremists, including beatings, burnings and bombings by the Ku Klux Klan and similar groups, but in the North, though such groups have sometimes been present at the fringes of some disorder, they have very rarely been constituent elements in its promotion. Violence related to housing grows out of our own native urban ignorance, perversity and lack of democratic responsibility.

Another cause of housing violence has been weak or corrupted police control.[12] Crowd situations and widespread hostility are the toughest of tests for police. Professional skill and strong commitment to duty are required to handle such problems. Police commanders who know that popular sentiment— and often, therefore, political sentiment—is against Negro occupancy in an area are reluctant to move with alacrity. Strong police morale and sympathetic leadership at some key points in the community structure are required if police control is to be effective. The rank-and-file policeman is hard pressed by the taunts of crowds which may be composed of his own neighbors. And he himself may fully share their anti-Negro outlook.

The complexities of race relations vex police personnel who are used to clear patterns of authority, action and judgment. There are many areas of gray with regard to the application of the law where illegal assembly, petty harassment and community expression are concerned which make the police unsure of their grounds for arrest or prosecution. In suburban areas, where there have been many incidents resulting from the first arrivals of Negroes in recent years, the police are frequently inadequate in both numbers and training to handle crowd agitation. In some cases state police are called in. In other cases the anti-Negro residents have their way and exert intense pressure upon the Negro newcomers.

People in urban society today are not accustomed to testing or baiting the police. When they do so, there is a novelty to the situation. The provocateurs are surprised to learn that they can escape without penalty for certain acts. Emboldened, they may go further. The pattern of illegal experiment begins, because the goal—the expulsion of an unwanted Negro family—is so much desired. There is in America a certain folk idea which holds authority in suspicion and reserves the right of the citizen to defy the guardians of law. Teen-age groups, at a stage when rebellion is second nature, frequently exploit exciting situations simply because they are exciting. The thrill of the moment is the object, and racial antagonism becomes only a convenient occasion.

The foregoing elements are the factors which, in proper combination, produce social conflict in areas of racial change in housing. A challenge to restrictions, a period of rising tension, aroused opinion and uncertain police control point toward outbreaks of property damage or attacks upon persons. In neighborhoods undergoing racial change the most dangerous situations arise when conditions are either extremely rigid or extremely fluid. If, for instance, a Negro spokesman has stated that a certain area, because of its long and vigilant resistance to Negro entry, is a special target, then lines of determined resistance may be drawn up. A rigid situation may develop, and the forces of resistance will close like a trap on any Negro family venturing into it. On the other hand, a Negro family may be moving into an area where all is confusion, wild emotion and distressed opinion. Leadership may be lacking, the police demoralized and the plans for the transfer of the property at loose ends. Such a situation provides the deranged or vindictive with a multitude of opportunities to do damage and excite fear. Either situation can deteriorate rapidly into violence.

We have said that most racial change takes place peacefully. How can this be if violence erupts in contested areas? Obviously not all situations contain the factors cited above disposing them toward violence. In addition, most racial change has been at the edge of the ghetto. Where there is not solid resistance surrounding the ghetto, there is often a resignation to racial change or at least a lack of resolution to fight it. Thus the ghetto is surrounded by both hard and "soft" spots. Penetration of the "soft" spots outflanks the "hard" areas. Most racial change in the last fifteen years has been a process of expansion of the ghetto at the edges. Such racial movement usually lacks the element of shock which marks the Negro entry into areas distant from the ghetto. The Negro who moves just beyond the rim of previous non-white occupancy also has a great number of his group not far away. This may be a significant deterrent to hostile action by whites. If a Negro family "jumps" to an outlying all-white area, however, they are isolated, symbolic, singled out by their uniqueness in the neighborhood and represent an intrusion for which the residents in all probability were completely unprepared.

Notable Cases

Aside from juvenile gang warfare, housing has been the steadiest source of urban racial violence in the North and West. As Charles Abrams has remarked, the reports from big-city race relations agencies have at times resembled communiques from some battlefront.[13] Some cases of attacks upon individual Negro families have been notable because they involved noted victims. In 1921 a celebrated case arose when Dr. Ossian Sweet, a physician, shot and killed a member of a mob attacking his home. The home of Dr. Percy Julian, co-discoverer of the miracle drug, cortizone, was bombed in Chicago in 1951. Most attacks are lost in the obscurity of the persons involved or are recorded on police blotters as "disturbance on the highway." There has been precious little study of these sporadic and transitory outbreaks. Large-scale riots and disorders have been studied. The pioneering work in this connection was the study of the 1919 Chicago riots by the Chicago Race Relations Commission. Many works of description and analysis have been carried out since then, but few of them deal with the disorders peculiar to housing.

If we review briefly some of the most notable riots centering on housing, we will be able to distinguish the major types of conflict in this area.

Probably the classic instance of civic irresponsibility and blundering was that which precipitated the Detroit riots in February 1942, involving the "Sojourner Truth" wartime housing project.[14] This situation reflected the strain of a community taxed at every point by the changes brought on by wartime activity. Government officials, having built a project and named it after a famous Negro abolitionist, changed their plans under the pressure of white politicians, residents and real estate men and refused to permit Negro occupancy. Then they switched again and leased the housing to Negroes. This was during a period of dire wartime housing shortage. The only unconfused force in the entire situation was the well-organized mob directed by a sound truck which met the first twelve Negro families. Pitched battles ensued when Negroes from the nearby Covent Gardens project came to the aid of the original twelve families. Finally the Negroes moved in under guard of armed militia. This riot was typical of the kind of eruption produced by the extreme pressure of a time of national crisis. Housing shortage, the mixture of people of different background, irresolute officials and unskilled police service marked the events.

In July 1951 a dispute between a landlord and tenants in Cicero, Illinois, outside Chicago, led to the rental of a unit to a Negro, a college graduate.[15] The resulting riots caused $20,000 damage to the property and could only be quelled when the state militia was called in. The local police and government officials behaved in a disgusting manner, abetting the mob, intimidating the Negroes and then whitewashing their role with a crude local grand jury report which blamed everybody but the local leaders and rampaging local residents for the outbreaks. A Federal judge ordered the local officials to uphold the law and the right of Negroes to occupy property. The Cicero riots revealed the ancient machinery of urban corruption involved with racial violence. The drama was a large-scale enactment of racial violence in older urban areas, where shady politicians and subservient police cynically overrule the law and conduct themselves in deference to anti-Negro prejudice.

In July 1953 a Negro mail-carrier moved into the Trumball Park Homes, a public housing project in Chicago.[16] Rumors spread, crowds gathered. After an initial wavering the police threw heavy forces into the area. The most determined kind of mob agitation took place. There were flares, fireworks, stones were thrown, and dozens of ingenious kinds of vandalism were let loose. The massive campaign of racial protest lasted for weeks. Hit-and-run demonstrators kept up their campaign for months. The Chicago Housing Authority moved other Negro families into Trumball Park during this period. The Negroes had to be escorted by police in and out of the area to shop, attend school or go to work. The nights were made hideous by fireworks, the wail of sirens and the screams of the rowdy crowds. Local civic associations and several neighborhood newspapers which turned into vicious anti-Negro sheets promoted the racist activity.

The Trumball Park riots severely tested the Chicago authorities. The police, the Housing Authority and the mayor were roundly criticized both by the supporters of housing desegregation and the anti-Negro elements. On the whole the authorities held firm. They supervised the placement of Negro families, tried to cope with the hostility and to hold the line against tremendous pressure. They made various mistakes, but on the whole they cannot be said to have failed in their duty.

The Trumball Park events constitute a pinnacle of urban residential violence. They represent a full-scale battle between urban racist opinion and public authority. These riots were most notable for their magnitude, their protracted span and the solidarity of the local elements promoting them. They were a more sustained campaign than the "Sojourner Truth" riots in Detroit or the Cicero outbreaks. The Trumball Park disorders are the kind of bitter, dogged, violent racial contests that public authorities fear most. Sudden, brief outbursts can be shattering to civic confidence and harmony, but long, fierce cycles of agitation are more expensive to the city budget and carry with them a greater possibility of political upheaval by white or Negro voters.

In the sixteen-thousand-home suburb of Levittown, Pennsylvania, in August 1957 one of the smart ranch houses was occupied by William Myers, a Negro skilled mechanic who worked at a refrigerator plant.[17] The new suburb had been sold by mass builder William Levitt to whites only. Myers had obtained a house from friends. Rumors went around that Communists were engineering the sale. Some of those close to Myers did have records of affiliation with groups on the Attorney General's list of subversive organizations. As the first Negro to enter the new town, which was populated by a mixture of white-collar families, skilled mechanics and workers in the new United States Steel plant nearby, Myers was bound to face trouble. Levitt and the housing bias system had created an all-white city. Many of the residents had taken on heavy mortgages in the new suburb to escape from racially mixed neighborhoods in Philadelphia. The arrival of a Negro was, they felt, a stab in the back by Levitt and a fantastic act of provocation by aggressive Negro organizations or Communists.

Crowds assembled around Myers' house, shouting and grumbling. Local police were forced to admit their inadequacy after several evenings of demonstrations. State police were called in. Several melees developed, and both police and demonstrators were injured. Mass meetings spawned a group of anti-Negro leaders who continued a harassment campaign from a house next to that of Myers, which they rented. Police were at first unsure of how to deal with this technique, since the antagonists were on private property, not in the street. The Attorney General of Pennsylvania had the malefactors haled into court and enjoined from continuing their harassment.

The Levittown disorders represent the kind of shocked reaction that has occurred in various suburbs in recents years when Negroes appeared. The suburbs have been the all-white sanctuary, and the entry of Negroes is infuriating to those who have fled from racial change in the central city areas. Typical in the Levittown situation was the inadequacy of local suburban police. Suburban police forces are often undermanned and subject to strong political control from the borough bosses. The formation of a number of pro-integration groups on the scene is also typical of the better-educated element, conscious of its civic responsibility, which resides in suburbia. A number of such groups arose to try to meet the problems which appeared in Levittown in August 1957.[18] Levittown, Pennsylvania, is a good case-study of racial change in suburbia. While it was more rowdy than situations involving Negro entry into other communities, it contained most of the forces typical of the all-white suburban communities ringing the nation's metropolitan centers.

Who, Us?

The foregoing instances represent the most notable kinds of violence arising out of residential change in or around our urban centers. These were the more dramatic of the recurrent frictions accompanying the racial movement which followed World War II. This kind of violence—and, of even greater weight, the threat of it—has an immense bearing on the question of housing mobility. This is seldom recognized—or admitted—by public officials and civic leaders. The significance of the physical peril involved in crossing racial barriers is played down for a number of reasons.

First, no urban community wants to be known as a violent community. Politicians and other leaders are quick to disclaim any sinister potential among their constituencies. Violence is against the formal ideology of tolerance in our civic life, whatever the hard codes of intolerance may be that shape everyday existence. Second, violence tests the civic and political structure and reveals its weaknesses. Urban leaders do not welcome such social tests. They fear any event that would expose widespread citizen prejudice, strategic police hostility or disruptive racial discords among key leadership groups. The power groups in a community, no matter what discords are present in their daily relationships, usually close ranks to prevent the exposure of such failings. Finally, as we have pointed out, the political leaders of urban communities fear violence because it could lead to political retaliation against them by one group or another. Machine politics proceed best in peace. Violence arouses deep resentment that may cause widespread racial consciousness to take hostile political form.

In the big cities, therefore, although there is much genuine liberal sentiment which abhors violence as an attack on the rights of all men, it is not so much a concern for individual dignity or humanitarianism that sets opinion against racial violence as it is the consensus of essentially cautious civic leadership that racial intimidation and vandalism are dangerous to leadership control and obstructive of business as usual and of their own pragmatic interests.

In addition to the significance that violence has for the leadership circles of the urban areas, it is also of great moment to the ordinary city residents who make housing changes. The threat of violence is even more significant than any actual event. Racial violence has tremendous emotional impact. Most burglaries, assaults, student riots and other outbreaks involve selected groups. But racial violence is felt to pertain to the whole population. Everybody has a skin color. The affinities are subtle but real. A publicized injury to a member of one or another racial group begets wide sympathy and attention in an almost automatic fashion in our racially conscious urban areas. It should be always remembered that the imagination tends to exaggerate pain, distress and confused events.

Many urban leaders are convinced that violence will immediately result from racial change in certain directions. So, although they may pay lip service to desegregation, they back
away from it if it becomes a practical issue. Housing desegregation especially arouses this fear. Rather than experiment, the
political and civic leaders support the status quo and maintain
the lines of residential demarcation.

The Incident Chasers

Important though the civil rights movement has been, the
fear of violence and disorder is probably the major reason why
one city after another has established a commission to deal
professionally with intergroup problems. Municipal intergroup
agencies such as those existing in New York, Chicago, Detroit,
Los Angeles and Philadelphia have developed various programs to deal with community tension that might lead to violence. Counter-measures against rumors; swift assertion of positive leadership in the event of a strained situation; the exercise
of peaceful religious and civic influences and liaison between
civic groups and police are part of such programs. In some
cities there are committees on community tension composed
of social workers, police, agency informants and others which
meet regularly to assess community conditions. In conjunction
with the official city government intergroup agencies, these
committees help keep a running tally of incidents, rumor waves
and events likely to produce agitation. This method of monitor-
ing community tensions in large cities has put the public authorities in a much better position for dealing with the continuous minor frictions which hold the potential for larger outbreaks. However, the effectiveness of the technique has been
impaired in most cities by the fact that the reporting has not
been on a broad enough base to assure the authorities full

knowledge of community irritations and small incidents. In addition, there is in most of the large cities a difficult problem of information and co-ordination between the various community agencies when some threatening situation arises. Bureaucracy is too clumsy for the swift pace of events.

Municipal intergroup agencies act on the assumption that cases of community friction and housing change take priority over educational or legal matters of less immediate importance. Recognizing the dangers of community hostility, the agencies seek to give prompt attention to neighborhood work to quell any disturbance. Moreover, their staffs try to evaluate trends in recreation, community activities and housing turnover in the effort to foresee problem situations. With respect to housing changes, this means that the staff must have considerable knowledge of actual non-white population distribution, housing market trends, the details of transactions and local neighborhood opinion.

There are three criteria commonly applied to housing cases for evaluation of violence potential. City authorities must inquire as to:

1.   What kind of incident or situation is involved? Cases of direct refusal to rent or sell a house are not usually violence-producing, although occasionally some vandalism might occur in connection with them. Actual racial change, the transfer of a property by agreement, is more often the provocation. Signs of trouble can be fears, rumors, inflammatory statements or plain confusion and curiosity among neighbors. Aggressive behavior may be covert and in the form of anonymous threats, phone calls, letters, harassment or vandalism. Open aggression may be through verbal provocation, crowd gatherings, assault, disorder, or actual riot. An incident may be complicated by panic selling of homes or exploitation by real estate men or extremist politicians.

2.   What is the location of the problem? Various neighborhoods have special attributes that call for careful attention.
These would be: (a) neighborhoods with histories of conflict,
i.e. with histories of labor struggle, juvenile gangs or anti-Negro
civic associations; (b) "pocket" neighborhoods, or "diehard"
neighborhoods, e.g. areas that are physically isolated, or areas
where resistance to change has been built up by encroachment;
(c) ethnic enclaves, where ethnic or foreign-language groups
have a high degree of solidarity and a cult of rejection of "out
groups" and (d) all-white areas where change comes unex-
pectedly. As we have said, areas removed from non-white concentrations may react with shock to racial change.

3.   What is the time of the incident or situation? There are
certain periods during which intergroup problems demand
special vigilance: *Weather* that permits outdoor activity and
increases the tempo of neighborhood social life is favorable to
rumor mongering, crowd gatherings, etc. Very hot weather
may make the situation more acute. *School Vacations*—juvenile actions relating to intergroup problems tend to rise during such periods. *Week-ends after move-ins*—week-ends after
minority families have taken possession of properties—perhaps
holiday week-ends in particular—give vandals or agitators an
opportunity to devote extra time to their work. *Periods of tense
public opinion*—times of civic crisis, when disasters or crimes,
strikes or other disorders have excited public unrest are periods when hostilities are likely to flare up. Times of severe
housing shortage require special vigilance.

Most city intergroup relations agencies have a system for
alerting the mass media concerning incidents. Chicago, Philadelphia and other cities have drawn up codes or "guide lines"
in conjunction with television, radio and newspaper personnel
in an effort to insure that news coverage of racial problems
shall not be inflammatory or in any other way irresponsible.[19]

The traditional tendency of news media to feature conflicts and sensationalize bizarre happenings in general is extremely difficult to overcome. In some cases, however, the newspapers decline to print notices of racial violence, perhaps because of their lack of a clear policy for the treatment of such news. It is a cardinal rule of intergroup practice to try to provide clear information to the news media so that their coverage can be based on facts. The importance of sustained attention to the media is not yet fully recognized in this field.

The more perceptive agencies have occasionally called on key persons to use their prestige to confirm respect for the law in troubled areas.[20] The use of influential local leaders to moderate opinion and reactions is a standard practice in disturbed situations. Direct field work by agency representatives co-ordinates the efforts of such leaders. Various arguments are used to build up a determination to avoid violence. One theme that can be strongly stressed is that violence may damage the innocent not only physically but psychologically and morally. Another argument hammered into responsible citizens is that vandalism and other violent outbreaks provide excitement for teen-agers and mentally disturbed persons. Once a taste of excitement has been had, there is an urge to prolong the thrilling experience. Violence, once started, cannot be easily stopped. In the neighborhoods most resistant to arguments based on civic responsibility, where respect for law is minimal, a self-interest argument can be used to preserve order among home owners who have a strong desire to sell their houses. It can be stressed that violence, by giving the area a "terror" reputation, will make property sales very difficult. These arguments based on primitive self-interest usually prove more effective than appeals to moral sanctions or the principles of democratic living. It is tragic that morality and democratic ethics do not constitute a stronger source of community peace and tolerance in urban society.

Police Training

Most intergroup relations agencies try to work closely with the police. Some participate in police training programs. Mutual exchange of information is worked out and conferences permit review of cases and consultation. The police commanders are usually concerned about the wider implications of racial violence, but the rank-and-file policemen tend to take a cynical view of the whole situation, regarding intergroup relations personnel as just another kind of confused and impractical social worker. The fact is that city police forces have in recent years found difficulty in recruiting officers according to high standards, since competition from other forms of employment has diminished the attractiveness of police work. The lower the educational attainment of the policeman, the harsher his racial attitudes are likely to be. In practically every major city, the attitudes of police and their treatment of Negroes have been a major public issue in the last several years.[21] Although communications and respect between intergroup relations professionals and police are growing and procedures for detecting and containing racial incidents improving, the picture is not yet a satisfactory one.

It will be seen from the foregoing that intimidation by violence has been a potent factor in retarding the penetration of the general housing market by minority families. The psychological significance of instances of riot or crowd assembly has been vastly disproportionate to the frequency of the incidents themselves, owing to the emotional quality of racial thinking. The threat of violence is the more insidious in its effects precisely because the actual occurrence is so erratic. Responsible civic forces must respond to it when and where it happens. Their only course is to encourage a complex preparedness and to be constantly alert.

Racial intimidation in the cities is a dire threat to our democracy. It is a primitive challenge to the rule of law and the dignity of the individual. It is a corrosive evil undermining moral ideals, especially when, in its more subtle forms, it is encouraged, connived at or instigated by political and civic leaders. Next to simple buying power and the discrimination of professionals in the housing industry, the presence or absence of intimidating threats and incidents has probably been the most important influence in determining alterations in the distribution of urban non-white population. This will not be the case in the future, but it has been so in the past.

NOTES

1. See Abrams, *Forbidden Neighbors*. See A. M. Lee and N. D. Humphrey, *Race Riot* (New York, The Dryden Press, 1943).
2. A. Raper, *The Tragedy of Lynching* (Chapel Hill, University of North Carolina Press, 1933).
3. Grimshaw, *op. cit.*
4. For an analysis of the difficulties of pioneer families, see Drayton Bryant and Thomas Colgan, "Some Problems of Pioneer Families in Changing Racial Patterns," *Journal of the National Association of Intergroup Relations Officials,* July 1958.
5. E. and E. Grier, *In Search for Housing* (New York, New York State Commission Against Discrimination, 1958), details Negro stress.
6. Dorothy Jayne, *First Families* (Philadelphia Commission on Human Relations).
7. For an analysis of working-class authoritarianism in this respect see S. Lipset, *Political Man* (Garden City, New York, Doubleday, 1960), ch. iv.
8. Grimshaw, *op. cit.*, p. 79.
9. *Ibid.*, p. 208.
10. The Philadelphia Commission on Human Relations had various cases of this type. In one, a Negro answering an advertisement to buy used furniture in a white area set off a rumor wave of housing change.

11. Hannah Lees, "How Philadelphia Stopped a Race Riot," *Greater Philadelphia Magazine,* November 1955; also Remarks of George Schermer, Director, Philadelphia Commission on Human Relations, before the Commission's Seminar for Mass Media, 1961.

12. An instance of such dereliction is told in Charles Abrams, "The Time Bomb that Exploded in Cicero," *Commentary,* November 1951.

13. Abrams, *Forbidden Neighbors,* p. 116.

14. Lee and Humphrey, *op. cit.*

15. The story of Cicero is told in Abrams, "The Time Bomb that Exploded in Cicero."

16. The Trumball Park Riots are well documented in the report of the Chicago Commission on Human Relations already cited, *The Trumball Park Homes Disturbances.*

17. The Levittown disorders are reported in *House and Home,* October 1957.

18. Report to the National Conference of Christians and Jews by John A. McDermott, Philadelphia Program Director, 1958.

19. The Chicago Commission on Human Relations devised a code of practice in 1960 in this respect. The Philadelphia Commission on Human Relations through a press seminar aroused mass media interest in the problem. See the Commission's Seminar for Mass Media, April 1960.

20. Jackie Robinson, for instance, has aided New York authorities in crisis situations on occasion.

21. Police Commissioner Kennedy in New York exchanged acid comment with Harlem Negro leaders in 1960. Detroit leaders forced a reorganization of the Commission on Human Relations, largely on the basis of police-community relations problems, in 1961. Philadelphia Negro leaders met angrily with the Mayor on police problems in April 1961.

7

Renewal and Rights

THE GREAT CITIES of the ancient world were built by slaves. The cities of the United States have been built by free men, but these men were not as free as they might have been. From ancient times it was the custom to partition cities, allotting portions to "foreigners," "aliens" and those who were to be exploited; there were always slums, vice districts and squalid quarters for outcasts. Occasionally they were emptied by wars or plagues, but as long as the cities endured, the misery of these slum areas endured. The dominant groups in the cities turned their attention to these districts when they became obnoxious or too inconvenient, but few men dreamed that such areas could actually be abolished and replaced with a decent and humane environment.

In democratic society the idea that the people themselves could change themselves and their living conditions eventually led to the idea that the people themselves, or their agents, could change the cities. The scabrous decay of the past and the disorder created by industrial life were made more evident as the level of education rose and depressions or wars brought community crisis to the cities. Urban leaders began to develop the notion that cities could be renewed and that the concentrated resources of democratic life and government could act to overcome the cycles of deterioration and discouragement that afflicted urban community life.

The first heralds of urban restoration and rebuilding were architects, philosophers and social scientists. British town planners tried experiments with government aid that impressed Americans. During the great economic collapse of the 1930's, the Federal Government experimented by building several well-planned towns. Far more significant, however, was the Federal effort to clear the slums. This activity was begun partly to provide homes in the 1930's for the ill-housed "one third of a nation" and partly as a "make work" program aimed at giving employment and priming the economy. The first units built were on land cleared of ramshackle tenements on New York's Lower East Side. Soon cities were competing for Federal grants to erect public housing projects.[1]

From its beginnings during the Great Depression, the public housing program developed into a pioneering movement of Federal activity in the field of housing. The experience gained in public housing work would serve as the precious seed for the nurture of urban renewal. Although the Federal Government would later extend its housing activity in many directions, it was low-rent public housing which developed the elementary techniques of slum survey, land acquisition and clearance, and housing construction which would serve as the foundation of urban renewal practice. It was also public housing that would provide Federal and municipal authorities with some rudimentary lessons in race relations, for many of the early projects were in heavily Negro old city areas.

As the city planning movement spread in the United States, the inadequacy of city living conditions was revealed in one area after another. The sheer size of the cities, their complexity and the demands of the more informed citizens for sensible controls and some degree of order brought planning commissions into existence. The establishment of official planning bodies, even if they were only advisory, was good public business and good politics. The housing shortage and curtailment of private building during World War II made the needs of urban communities starkly evident even to those who opposed Federally sponsored action. The immense changes induced by the war and the post-war migrations forced municipalities to evaluate their physical and social needs. In the post-war years the concept of redevelopment took form. Redevelopment was more than slum clearance.[2] It was a broader program of replanning and rebuilding entire neighborhoods to make them conform to good city-planning design. This work, undertaken by local agencies with varying degrees of autonomy and skill, was the first large-scale entry of the city-planning movement into the turmoil of old city neighborhoods. To redevelopment was added the expanded concept of broad-scale urban renewal, which included not just physical rebuilding, but social reorganization at various levels of life. Some even saw the renewal system as a permanent feature of urban life, continuing its function of rebuilding just as the police, water and transportation services went on constantly meeting changing demands.[3]

It became very clear during the 1950's that urban renewal was a considerable force for displacing population and changing patterns of residence. In one city after another the griefs of displaced families made headlines. The physical displacements gave rise to social complications which baffled public agencies, to the extent that relocation of occupants from sites to be rebuilt became the Achilles heel of the urban renewal process. Moving people was complicated, vexatious and politically perilous.

The blossoming of the urban renewal movement occurred in the late 1950's. This was the same decade in which the great

urban centers were awakening to the significance of vast increases in their non-white populations. As we have seen, these
developments were linked in the central city areas. Urban renewal became involved with civil rights problems at a time
when the civil rights of Negroes were a burning national issue.
Since the urban renewal process had developed rapidly and
somewhat fitfully, the full social significance of the process in
relation to such problems as race relations had not been clearly
recognized by the local agencies spurring renewal programs.
But now it soon became obvious that little progress would be
made unless the more severe racial complaints caused by renewal could be dealt with.

Legal Promises

The phalanx of agencies working to rebuild worn-out urban
areas in some places had legal instruments to guide their involvement with race relations problems. In some states there
were non-discrimination clauses written into redevelopment
acts and contracts. A number of cities had imposed such
clauses. These legal restraints slowly began to shape policy.
Ten states had statutes that applied to urban redevelopment
specifically.[4] Non-discrimination clauses affecting public housing had been the thin end of the legal wedge in most cases.
Public housing for low-income families was the first kind of
residential renewal in many cities. Private developers in the
1940's and the early 1950's were usually unwilling to try their
hand at redevelopment work. The cleared land that had previously been occupied by slums was picked up by public housing authorities for low-rent projects. Thus the first redevelopment projects were often heavily Negro, low-rent developments.
"Non-discrimination" often meant heavily or totally Negro oc-

cupancy, because public housing was serving Negroes to an ever growing extent in large urban areas.

Non-discrimination laws affecting urban renewal work were later extended in some states like New York and New Jersey to cover "government-aided housing," i.e. houses built with mortgages guaranteed by the FHA, the VA, or state housing finance agencies.[5] In Pennsylvania the Redevelopment Act of 1945 had extended non-discrimination protection by ordaining a covenant running with the redeveloped land for this purpose. Such laws usually extended protection not only to housing but to facilities built on redeveloped land (schools, recreation centers, etc.). In 1959 the Federal Housing and Home Finance Agency required that housing built to accommodate families displayed by renewal work be sold without discrimination.[6] The tax-supported effort to promote urban rebuilding was being increasingly provided with legal guides that barred racial restrictions.

As the legal coverage of urban renewal activity was being expanded, the administrative machinery for assuring enforcement of anti-discrimination laws was also growing. State and city agencies responsible for enforcing the laws were gaining increased competence throughout the 1950's. Public housing was gradually implementing non-discrimination policy. In 1952 twenty states had open occupancy policies in public housing. By 1960 this number had grown to thirty-two states with 59.6% of the Housing Authorities reporting some Negro occupancy.[7] Intergroup relations personnel were on the staffs of government agencies at all levels. Experience and legal precedent were growing.

The government agencies and responsible civic circles promoting urban renewal recognized the injustice of rebuilding for only part of the public. Non-discrimination laws were an attempt to insure that renewal benefits would extend to all of

the public. The task of overcoming restrictive practices was
not easy. Business elements decried the added legal commitments involved in urban renewal, and non-discrimination laws
rubbed such groups raw. But the government agencies could
no longer flagrantly disregard Negro rights and injuries. To do
so was bad politics. The civil rights organizations, church
groups and Negro constituencies wanted at least a legal commitment to fair treatment. The formal ideology of democracy
also could not be ignored. A national movement to revitalize
urban life had to defer to the democratic principles underlying
government service and civic morality. A fundamental consideration was the fact that slum clearance and urban renewal
programs were operating in the central city areas occupied by
minority groups and could thus be witnessed and judged by
these groups at first hand.

The non-discrimination policy of much of the urban renewal network was also shaped by the necessity for the urban
centers to alleviate bad living conditions in minority neighborhoods purely from self-interest. Improvement had to proceed
if the central cities were to be competitive with the suburban
areas. It could not proceed unless Negroes were accorded the
benefits of the renewal process. The inadequate living standards and cultural privations in lower-class Negro neighborhoods were a threat to the social and economic livelihood of
the cities. The relaxation of racial restrictions, therefore, was
motivated by self-interest on the part of many civic leaders who
strongly supported urban renewal. This, as much as the increased momentum of legal developments in civil rights or the
growing political strength of Negroes, was a spur in shaping
anti-discrimination policy.

The carrying out of desegregation within the framework of
urban renewal programs in the major cities has been uneven
and fraught with difficulties. While the line of legal and policy

developments has been increasingly clear, the actual implementation of these policies in desegregation and open-occu-
pancy programs has been an increasingly muddled affair. Certain problem areas have become quicksands of negotiation,
postponement and compromise. One of these problems has
involved site selection for new buildings.

Segregated Sites

In many cities the front running agencies in the application
of non-discrimination laws have been the local public Housing
Authorities. These agencies, serving a heavily Negro, low-
income clientele, have been vaguely co-ordinated with the over-
all planning activities. Criticism of massive public housing
projects concentrated in limited geographical areas had induced some Authorities to try to disperse their building programs. Dispersing public housing sites would mean cheaper
land costs, better design of projects and, most important, a
reduction of population density in the crowded, heavily Negro,
old city areas. It would also mean placing Negroes in heretofore
all-white neighborhoods. Public housing projects have been accorded a cool welcome in many neighborhoods because of the
problem families involved, but public housing with mixed racial occupancy meets rigidly frozen resistance in white neighborhoods. In Chicago, site selection for public housing without regard to existing racial patterns ran into furious resistance.
The Chicago City Council instituted a "containment" policy
in response to political pressures to keep public housing in the
heavily Negro areas.[8] In 1956, when the civic groups interested
in sound planning joined the Housing Authority in Philadelphia in proposing twenty-one sites scattered throughout the
city, many in all-white neighborhoods, there was an uproar.

The proposal was a move to free public housing from its increasingly segregated pattern of Negro concentration and to reduce the density in the older neighborhoods undergoing urban renewal. The resulting furor was a classic donnybrook of opinion clashes. After a hurried tour of sites, the City Councilmen worried the proposal and worked for further study of sites.[9] The result has been that practically all sites since 1956 have been in Negro neighborhoods.

In Cleveland in 1960 the Housing Authority began to cast its eyes on a large tract of land on the west bank of the Cuyahoga River. The tract required rezoning. When residents of the area got news of the Authority's rezoning attempt they reacted bitterly against the prospect of an influx of Negro neighbors in the proposed multi-story development. The plans were balked.[10] Thus the efforts of planners to use public housing to reduce central city densities and ease renewal have been hamstrung in one place after another. In many cases the complaints that public housing brings problem families are understandable. Social work to improve such families has lagged in public housing projects and elsewhere. But angry expressions of racial antagonism have been more notable in the campaigns against public housing at the local level.

Relocation Wrangles

Another feature of urban renewal with deep implications for racial change has been the relocation of families from renewal sites. The displacing of families for slum clearance and redevelopment projects is a controversial activity at best, but when these families are mostly Negro, the issue becomes explosive. To rehouse displaced families adequately requires that a broad range of housing choices be available. Racial restrictions de-

limit the range of choices for such families. The agencies responsible for relocation work are confronted with a well-nigh
insoluble problem: finding adequate housing for displaced
families without disturbing racial patterns to the extent of producing a public uproar. Displaced families from slum sites do
not usually make the best pioneers in the movement of penetrating all-white neighborhoods. They tend to have too many
problems and too low a morale to face the stress involved in
such ventures.

In addition to the fact that conscientious relocation means
defying racial restrictions in the housing market, the whole
subject of relocation has been a prime target for charges of
mismanagement, exploitation and discrimination. The moving
of families at government instigation goes somewhat against the
grain of the American. The social complications involved in
moving the ill, the aged, the unemployed, families distressed
by many problems and families who do not want to move are
staggering.

Redevelopment officials engaged in the actual task of trying
to find standard housing within the means of families displaced
by public action are caught in the over-all web of housing discrimination. Most relocation offices must rely on the co-operation of real estate brokers and agents who provide information
about housing vacancies so that displaced families can be referred to them. These brokers and agents receive "finder's fees"
in many cities. But realty men firmly refuse to defy racial boundaries in referring vacancies. Relocation officials also state that
poor Negro families will break off contact with relocation offices if they are referred to dwellings and apartments by the
office only to have the door slammed in their faces by bigoted
landlords. In some cases in which Negroes have been found
alternative dwellings in white areas, there have been wholesale
moveouts by whites. The result has been not the constructive

use of relocation to further desegregation but the furtherance of segregation trends at the edge of the ghetto.

In one city after another the displacement of Negroes and the attempts of public officials to seek new locations for them within the segregation system has led to an aggravation of housing problems and the exacerbation of race relations. In Pittsburgh redevelopment pushed Negroes out and resulted in overcrowding in adjacent areas.[11] In Philadelphia only three out of ten displaced families, who were largely Negro, were obtaining dwellings that met Housing Code standards of decency and safety, and the displaced families had to pay an average of 10% more rent for these alternate units.[12] In Washington, D.C., low-income Negroes were moved out and high-income units built, but the displaced families had to scrabble for public housing units or whatever else was in supply.[13] In Chicago the Urban League claimed that the Negro housing problem had actually become worse in the years of urban renewal growth.[14] The situation was bad enough to send at least one Congressman, Representative Frank Thompson of New Jersey, on a rampage in Congress over the cavalier course of urban renewal and relocation.[15]

Priced Out

Another way in which urban renewal has nullified the high policy pronouncements of non-discrimination is through the economic exclusion of non-whites, who are preponderantly in the lower-income brackets. The issue of equality of opportunity to buy or rent units resulting from urban renewal is academic if non-whites are "priced out of the market." Housing built for upper-income markets excludes Negroes almost as effectively as housing built under strict segregationist codes.

To the biting effect of racial rejection, real or imagined, is added the still graver injustice that the homes of the poor have been demolished to permit the erection of luxury towers for the well-to-do. In Cincinnati, Chicago and Washington renewal programs have ousted Negro poor to erect upper-income projects.[16]

Urban renewal in the early 1960's is beginning to attract private capital. Business-sponsored projects are not likely to be devoted to low-income housing, or even moderate-income housing. Serving rich whites and displacing poor Negroes is a dangerous temptation that could take on tragic dimensions and make renewal the target for large-scale Negro wrecking efforts.

Because urban renewal has worked within the framework of the segregation system, altering this system only in marginal ways, the policy pronouncements about non-discrimination have become suspect in the minority community. Urban renewal has, as yet, had little real impact on the pattern of housing segregation. The all-important decisions about site selection and the economic range of developments have resulted in containing Negroes within the segregated areas. The decline in the reputation of public housing has led Negroes to conclude that the low-rent projects are second-rate housing. The one type of housing generally open to Negroes in renewal areas is viewed by whites and by many Negroes as a quarantine system of low-rent compounds specializing in wrecked families. The vexatious problem of relocation, with its examples of distressed families and evicted elderly people, has had a further adverse affect upon the attitude of minority groups toward urban renewal programs.

Segregation Renewed?

The net impact of urban renewal thus far has been to alleviate some of the worst housing conditions within the ghetto
areas, but at the price of visiting physical and social dislocation
upon those least able to cope with it. The detrimental effects of
renewal have not simply been experienced by minority families
as by other families; they have been felt by these families in
spite of pledges, proclamations and pious pronouncements designed to reassure them. And, very importantly, these difficulties and contrasts under the urban renewal program have fitted
into the traditional pattern of misfortune that the Negro has
been conditioned to expect. They serve to confirm his worst
misgivings about distinctions between racial groups. It seems
patent to many Negro leaders that although some of the benefits of renewal in the form of public housing have gone to Negroes, the burdens and afflictions of the program have fallen
preponderantly and disproportionately upon them.[17] The increased participation of private financial interests in urban
renewal programs will mean more emphasis on "safe" profit
schemes for commercial and industrial renewal. If renewal has
been tolerable while exercised in the cause of better housing, it
may not be so tolerantly accepted when it works on behalf of
private corporations and commercial combines.

Despite these rather pessimistic implications, urban renewal
represents an important social fulcrum for the Negro populations of the urban areas. It would be premature to identify city
rebuilding with misfortune for Negroes. The renewal system is
actually just emerging. Twenty years ago there were hardly any
examples of renewal—early slum clearance was a hit-or-miss,
piecemeal affair. Today a powerful, nation-wide city restoration movement is underway, of which we have thus far seen

only the first phase. The most important precedents are set in favor of eventual equality of treatment and opportunity for Negroes. Geography, the law and the political facts of life all point in this direction. The bureaucrats may thus far have shrewdly baffled flexible renewal plans to avoid Negro mobility. They may have made the relocation problem worse, but the future of non-discrimination is ordained. It is the effects of the guarantee that are questionable.

The basic physical fact we have constantly stressed, that Negroes are concentrated in and around the central city renewal areas, dictates that they will be more and more deeply involved in the rebuilding process as clientele, critics and administrators.[18] The legal safeguards that today seem somewhat flimsy will become stronger as precedents grow, provisions become clearer and pressure rises to insure enforcement. These trends, coupled with mounting Negro political power, mean that Negro participation in urban renewal is just beginning.

The economic lag that excludes Negroes from the upper-income housing which is filling cleared sites will not soon be overcome. The bulk of the minority housing market will remain oriented toward moderate and low-income dwellings. Where job opportunities have provided steady income, Negroes have demonstrated strong home-buying propensities. It is not new housing, therefore, that offers the best field for Negro participation in urban renewal, but the rehabilitation of existing housing. Racially mixed neighborhoods in Detroit, Chicago, Philadelphia and Washington, D.C., have been the scene of active programs to keep housing standards high. Home-owning Negroes have amply demonstrated their interest in maintaining good neighborhood conditions in selected areas.[19] The spread of interest in housing rehabilitation and neighborhood organization throughout the Negro urban population could work a momentous change in living conditions in the older city areas.

Conservation and Civic Life

The first thrust of urban renewal has been toward the worst sore-spots of neighborhood decay. Bulldozer clearance and massive reconstruction have been immensely expensive, but these tactics have shown that something could be done to redeem central city land. City fathers are recognizing increasingly, however, that clearance of slums alone is not the answer to their most acute problems. Conservation of those portions of the housing supply that can be protected is now commanding more attention. The vast investment in capital facilities, both public and private, in the central cities demands that areas of decent residential life be maintained. The real estate tax base of the cities is at stake. Residential conservation is a necessity for the preservation of the urban economic and social order.[20]

The older neighborhoods where conservation efforts are needed are called the urban "gray zones." The quality of housing in these areas is mediocre; neither high-standard nor slum. In many cities the housing in the central city gray zones was built prior to 1920. It is poorly planned, tending toward obsolescence and open to exploitation by overcrowding on the part of owners who wish to obtain high returns. These gray zone districts are often the areas of jaded elegance or the neighborhoods in which immigrants liberated from various ethnic ghettos arrived at higher status. Today the melting of the segregation glaciers in the worst central city areas has brought Negroes into the gray zone. The effort to conserve the urban housing supply will in future years take place in middle-aged neighborhoods that will be either all-Negro or well-mixed in occupancy. It would not be overstating the case to say that the movement to save the centers of our metropolitan areas hinges upon the engagement of the Negro populations in the process.

The first reports from urban renewal authorities concerning community conservation activity in Negro areas have been encouraging.[21] Despite the history of severe privation and disorganization behind them, Negroes seem to be responding positively to the old magic of American status striving. Home ownership, civic organizations and leadership among them are increasing. The experience of home ownership in the lower levels of the housing market is strengthening Negro families. Competence and confidence are growing. The entire structure of public housing, middle-income projects and conservation activities is acting as a conditioning system that will increase the potential for desegregation. This is a long-term development, but it is real. It will be one of the wellsprings for revitalizing our urban life.

The urban renewal process is not only a social elevator with respect to housing; it has much deeper implications. Eventually it will involve a sustained private and public movement of expanded opportunity and community organization.[22] By reorganizing the physical environment of urban centers, it will open up broad areas of social change. Family life, civic participation and institutional development will all have the chance for improvement as the process goes on. The rebuilding of urban life may be the first great opportunity for Negroes to make a decisive historical contribution to American life, not from some marginal, minority position, but from within the mainstream of the most vital centers of our cultural life, the cities.

The urban renewal process injects something new into our society. The simple ideal of town-meeting democracy is not workable in the huge, complex cities; a new concept of community expression and democratic civic leadership is required. The urban renewal program has called for the development of new media and forms for local life—citizens' councils with paid staffs, advisory groups of technicians, locally chartered neighborhood development corporations have come into existence to deal with its problems. All these community agencies have broken new ground in civic organization.[23] They are privately sponsored and directed. They are the beginnings of a new, more responsible way of life in the cities. Clothed with tradition and with years of success behind them, these groupings can transform our urban ways from disorderly individualism and laissez-faire exploitation into a balanced system of representative social life.

The active engagement of Negroes in the evolution of this new urban society seems assured. Segregation can hinder, but it cannot preclude, the development of the Negro potential. The social opportunities presented by the new developments will be extended whether or not large-scale desegregation takes place. The interest of the cities in guaranteeing a decent environment and a stable economic base will continue. The persistence of the ghetto will modify the Negro contribution, but it cannot exclude it, for the churches, civic groups and families within the segregated neighborhoods will insist upon advancing their residential and civic standards.

The Goals of Renewal

To admit that urban renewal will probably proceed even if desegregation is not broadly successful does not minimize the logical necessity of full-fledged mobility for minorities. Urban renewal is merely one sphere of a larger social arena. It will be more difficult to accomplish if substantial desegregation does not take place. The density of the old city areas must be dispersed without regard to race. The economic and social imperatives which endorse desegregation do not derive from urban renewal needs alone, but from the need for freedom of choice as a stimulant for the economy, from the need to utilize our whole manpower in a time when our society is under the stress of keen competition. If flexible vitality is to be achieved in our metropolitan life, outmoded racial restrictions must be abandoned in favor of a higher civility and the ethic of democracy. The moral root-sytem of our society also craves a just solution to racial inequalities. Whether we meet the test of this larger impetus toward desegregation may be determined by how well we adapt the urban renewal movement to the expansion of minority housing opportunities and the desegregation of the central city areas.

If urban renewal programs are to be used to offset the social disabilities of the non-white populations and to effect gradual desegregation, these twin objectives must be made the goals of practical planning decisions. Extremely difficult judgments are involved. At the present time city planners and renewal officials are making choices between various kinds of renewal activity. Federal and local funds simply are not available to meet all the needs. Choices must be made between plans for residential or commercial and industrial or institutional rebuilding. There are no clear guide-lines as to which type of renewal is in the best interests of the city as a whole. Nor are there criteria as to which kinds of projects benefit the non-white population most. But the question of the kinds of projects which will most effectively counter the influence of segregation must be carefully considered. If the urban renewal program is inevitably to be immersed in the racial problem by virtue of its geographical application to the older city areas, it must weigh this issue.

Industrial and commercial redevelopment is necessary to make inner-city industry competitive with new suburban facilities. For the minority population the redevelopment which provides job training and fair employment opportunities is extremely important. Earning power is a key to family stability and to housing choice. And yet, industrial and commercial redevelopment can mean destruction of housing that is not replaced. It can mean speculative business schemes. It can mean indefinite postponement of slum clearance and of the direct benefits to family life that better housing could provide.

Institutional redevelopment such as that which expands school and university and other cultural facilities can also be of special benefit to minority citizens. One of the greatest means of unlocking the potential of minority groups is encouraging, and providing the opportunities for, education. The increase in the population and other new demands on the American educational system are tightening educational standards just when Negroes are most in need of rapid educational advances to meet the requirements of technical society. Automation and new industrial techniques are eliminating many jobs in the unskilled and semi-skilled categories. Negroes must have access to more educational service if they are to survive the pressures of these forces. More and broader educational facilities easily accessible to minority families can have a profound effect upon the social life of racial groups.

Residential renewal can of course relieve the most severe pressures on Negro community life. New housing makes a very attractive political objective. It infuses confidence and raises morale in depressed minority areas. The process of residential renewal, as we have said, gives new impetus to community organization and expression. Certainly the immediate relief which better housing provides for family life is fundamental in rectifying social disorders in minority life. But such immediate benefits can only interfere with the achievement of social stability through improved employment and educational opportunities.[24]

Strategy

The broad strategy of urban renewal in many places is taking its present shape in conformity with city budget problems. As we have already observed, the tax bases of the center cities, the hearts of the metropolitan areas, are in danger, and the reflex action of the business power groups is to chart a rescue program which will preserve the business establishment. The public administrators and politicians are not ill-disposed toward the monumental steel and aluminum architecture of downtown commercial renewal. It restores public confidence and fattens tax rolls. Thus a clear assessment of the impact of urban renewal on the long-term social prospects of the enlarging non-white populations is obstructed. Fiscal peril and the evidence of the social problems in the slums occupy the foreground of the planners' vision, crowding out a true social evaluation of racial prospects.

There is nothing malicious about this; in fact it is largely unconscious. The solution to the problem and the puzzle of segregation taxes the intellectual powers of the most sophisticated. Such considerations tend to be postponed. The work of restoring the cities has been exciting to the planners, the technical elite and even the bureaucrats and politicians. They have been preoccupied by the immense scope of their practical planning. In addition, the planners are very sensitive to charges of socialistically exceeding their authority in raising issues of a fundamental nature. Many planners shun such involvement and content themselves with doing, so to speak, the bread-and-butter work of highway and public-housing planning. Negro leaders have not fully appreciated the adaptation of minority group life to the urban sphere. Harassed with a multitude of other problems, the Negro intelligentsia has not comprehended the historic scope of the urban change.[25]

The dynamics of urban renewal may never really permit a rational, statesmanlike approach to its use as a remedy for minority privations in more than an immediate physical sense.[26] The positive use of the renewal program as a lever for desegregation may also not be considered or worked out. Americans have a headlong way of doing things which often precludes thorough planning for the future. But the pressure of increased population and the welfare state make sound social choices immensely important.

It would perhaps be too much to expect our urban society to respond to the persistent racial problem with a concerted long-range approach. Only in the field of law do we seem to be establishing enduring judgments. What we can practically plan for is avoiding the worst mistakes in the relationship between urban renewal and racial problems. Minority families must not be abused because they are relatively defenseless in face of the powerful redevelopment system. The system must not be captured by those elements in government, politics or commerce who have not taken in the emergency presented by our racial difficulties. If we can avoid these pitfalls, we can have some hope that the lively American tradition of freedom and social flexibility will reaffirm itself in our times of urban expansion.

Outside the South, where the principles of racism have been incorporated in the law, segregation has been operative without state sanction. But if the subtle, geographic segregation which has been taking place in our expanding cities is frozen onto the landscape, this will have to be done with the conscious complicity of government, for government today is not so remote as it was in the life of the old South. In the sphere of urban change, there is state intervention at every turn. Segregation is so much at variance with democratic practice that it can be sustained in our rapidly changing city life only with state endorsement, covert or overt. The urban renewal program affords the first major opportunity for us to see how well our Federal, state and local governments will measure up to the challenge of urban segregation. The unity and stability of our metropolitan centers may rest upon the outcome of this trial.

NOTES

1. Timothy McDonnell, *The Wagner Act* (Chicago, Loyola University Press, 1957).
2. President John F. Kennedy made this clear in his 1961 message to Congress on Housing.
3. See C. Woodbury, *The Future of Cities and Urban Redevelopment* (Chicago, University of Chicago Press, 1953); 2 vols.
4. A. Forster and S. Rabkin, "The Constitutionality of Laws Against Discrimination in Publicly Assisted Housing," *New York Law Forum,* January 1960, p. 41.
5. *Ibid.,* p. 43.
6. Directive of the Commissioner of the Housing and Home Finance Agency, August 14, 1959.
7. Housing and Home Finance Agency, Public Housing Administration, Intergroup Relations Branch, *Trends Toward Open Occupancy in Low-Rent Programs of the Public Housing Administration* (June 1, 1960).
8. See M. Meyerson and E. Banfield "Politics, Planning and the Public Interest," *The Case of Public Housing in Chicago* (Glencoe, Ill., The Free Press, 1955).
9. *The Philadelphia Evening Bulletin,* April 17, 1956.
10. *House and Home,* April 1961, p. 71.
11. Pittsburgh Commission on Human Relations, *The Status of Housing of Negroes in Pittsburgh* (November 1958).
12. The Philadelphia Housing Association, *Relocation in Philadelphia* (1958).
13. Rev. Robert C. Howes, *Crisis Downtown, A Church-Eye View of Urban Renewal* (Washington, D.C., National Catholic Welfare Conference, 1958).

14. *Urban Renewal and the Negro in Chicago* (Chicago, Chicago Urban League, 1958).

15. *Congressional Record,* February 21, 1961.

16. Staughton Lynd, "Urban Renewal for Whom?" *Commentary,* January 1961.

17. See the Report of the Housing Office of the National Association for the Advancement of Colored People: *Urban Renewal or Urban Removal* (1959).

18. Dennis Clark, "Urban Renewal and Intergroup Relations," *Journal of the National Association of Intergroup Relations Officials,* Winter 1961.

19. ACTION Housing, Inc., and the Housing and Home Finance Agency have published reports on such areas.

20. The Hon. Joseph S. Clark in the *New York Times Magazine,* May 2, 1961. See also Professor George Raymond in the April 1960 *Journal of Housing* on the need for "continuous renewal."

21. See *Interracial Review,* May 1961.

22. One survey showed substantial urban renewal programs in forty-eight cities. See R. Hemdahl, *Urban Renewal* (New York, The Scarecrow Press, 1960).

23. Citizen participation in urban renewal has been strong in Detroit, Chicago, Philadelphia and New Haven. Local groups have developed skillful information and participation programs. See *Citizen Participation in Neighborhood Conservation and Rehibilitation,* ACTION Housing, Inc., 2 Gateway Center, Pittsburgh, Pa.

24. N. Foote *et al., Housing Choices and Constraints* (New York, McGraw, 1960), says that the dispersal of a fair number of Negroes from the central city is necessary if renewal is to succeed (p. 214).

25. Robert Weaver, in an article, "Class, Race and Urban Renewal," *Land Economics,* August 1960, states that class may be replacing race as the decisive factor in urban renewal. If he is correct, the future of Negroes under the urban renewal program, then, would be influenced by class.

26. Foote *et al., op. cit.,* says: "The impact of the Negro on the housing market, by his presence in increasing numbers in the city, is obviously a crucial problem for him and for the future survival of the city. Thus far it shows few signs of rational resolution." (P. 129.)

8

The Order of Tolerance

IN THE PAST the main leaders in our society who were committed to the cause of justice to the Negro have had to contend with fundamentally anti-social and vicious practices which imposed themselves with a primitive force upon minorities. Dealing with first things first—slavery, lynching, racial terrorism, wholesale exploitation of Negro labor—left little time for long-term speculations about eventual desegregation and social unity. Men such as Marcus Garvey or W. E. B. DuBois did look far into the future and saw greatly varying prospects, but most leaders confined themselves to the effort of ameliorating the punitive aspects of racism and the crippling effects of segregation. In the second quarter of this century, however, leaders in the civil rights field and in Negro organizations became firmly committed to the full thesis of desegregation. This commitment has long existed in germinal form, but the great non-white migrations have occasioned its growth and development.

Mobility begot desegregation in both the practical and intellectual spheres. The rising educational level of the public and the general discourse evoked by events and mass communications have permitted the arguments for desegregation to reach a broad audience. In the last twenty years this audience, which has largely been a racially mixed elite urban group, has begun to take practical steps to popularize and to implement desegregation. Through the legislatures and courts, through political and educational groups and a wide variety of specialized civil rights and community relations activities, the movement for desegregation has pressed forward.

The impact of this movement upon race relations in the Northern and Western cities has been decisive. The movement has provided a rationale for the racial changes which the cities have been undergoing and has in some degree been a spur to these changes. Through civic leadership and educational activity it has sought to construct an order of tolerance in the tumultuous social life of the racially changing urban areas.

The desegregation of public and community facilities has progressed rapidly since 1940. The more complex changes in the sphere of employment are moving at a slower pace. The desegregation of residential life has, as of the early 1960's, resulted in a stalemate, with intermittent changes occurring at various strategic levels of community life, but with restrictive practices in housing still prevalent and in effective control of population movement.

Fair Housing Laws

The cutting edge of the civil rights movement has been the attempt to open new opportunities for minority group members. In the field of housing this has meant the adoption of fair housing laws. In the previous chapter legal prohibitions against discrimination as they affected redevelopment and urban renewal were discussed. Some of the state anti-discrimination measures cover not only redevelopment housing but houses built with other forms of government aid, whether state or Federal. Some of the laws go even further and cover portions of the private housing market as well.[1] The enforcement of such laws is lodged with the public agencies which also administer public accommodations and fair employment practice laws.

The affirmative use of law to overcome racial restrictions on the sale and lease of property is the reverse of the use of law to restrict property holding. The utilization of the law has required not only the definition of rights and duties according to justice, but the instruction of the citizenry in public policy with regard to race relations. In addition, the law is supposed to change actions, and eventually to change thinking, in the field of race relations. One expert affirms that not only can the law change race relations but ". . . that sometimes it has been indispensable to changing them, and that it has in fact changed them, even spectacularly."[2] In the campaign for residential desegregation this statement is less true than in other civil rights areas, but it is still valid.

The administrative and enforcement experience of cities and states operating with fair housing laws has been brief. New York City's law became effective in April 1958; Pittsburgh's in June 1959. New York State, Colorado, Connecticut, Washington, Oregon, Massachusetts, New Jersey and Pennsylvania all have had laws in effect for similar brief periods. To judge from the experience of Pittsburgh and New York, the effect of the laws is likely to be quite gradual. The purchase of housing and leasing of apartments are complicated matters. The pitfalls are many, and the hazards of obtaining legal redress against discrimination are manifold. The tricks of the real estate business, the technical requirements of the investigation of complaints by government agencies and the difficulties of obtaining satisfaction from a testy landlord all militate against prompt redress. Complainants under the laws have been rather scarce. Families find it easier to hunt for housing within the ghettos than to become engaged in slow and tedious investigative hearings and conferences. The laws are operative for those families able and aggressive enough to avail themselves of them,[3] but the proportion of such families in the minority communities is growing only gradually.

The Impact

The significance of the fair housing laws does not yet lie in their enforcement. They will have an increasingly important effect on desegregation as their use by complainants grows, but their current value is rather in their educational effect than in the opening up of broad areas of housing to Negro occupancy. Their very existence states public policy and makes socially respectable the sale of property which has previously been restricted; it serves also to detract from the concept of the exclusive, all-white community, with the result that the possibility of Negro entry can be discussed in practical terms in areas where residents would otherwise be implacably prejudiced or oblivious of the issue. In addition, the homebuilder, real estate broker and mortgage banker must now become more realistic about serving Negro housing demand. They can now point out to their white clientele that they must respect the law. To a considerable extent, therefore, such laws help to resolve the dilemma in the housing industry produced by immovable white opinion and advancing Negro housing demand.

A second most notable effect of the fair housing laws is that they are setting highly strategic legal precedents. The administrative and court decisions under such laws are puncturing the myth that the statutes are unconstitutional. The legal profession is becoming more aware of the reality of the laws in particular terms. This, in turn, will undoubtedly promote legal advice to real estate brokers and homebuilders favoring a cautious and rational approach to cases under the law.

From the case of Dorsey vs. Stuyvesant Town Corporation, in which a New York court held that in the absence of specific legislation an owner may discriminate in the sale or lease of property, the wheel of legal emphasis has come full circle.[4] An early case even held that a public Housing Authority could follow what was termed "the neighborhood pattern" in determining the racial composition of housing projects—i.e., white projects in all-white areas, mixed occupancy in mixed areas and segregated projects in all-Negro areas.[5] The most conclusive initial reversal of this earlier judicial tendency to prefer property rights and the racial status quo over human rights was in a case arising out of the enforcement of the New York State fair housing law. In the case of the New York State Commission against Discrimination vs. Pelham Hall Apartments, Justice Samuel Eager held that in a conflict between human rights and property rights, the power of the state to regulate the use and enjoyment of property in the interest of public welfare, when reasonably exercised, is supreme.[6] The New York law was thus held to be reasonable and constitutional. Of still greater import as far as the housing industry was concerned was the decision of the New Jersey Superior Court upholding the New Jersey law forbidding discrimination in housing built with FHA and VA mortgage guarantees.[7] The law being enforced on behalf of a Negro complainant by the New Jersey Division against Discrimination involved an appeal of the Division's decision by Levitt and Sons, one of the nation's largest homebuilders. This case spelled out in unmistakable terms the future of housing sales in states having fair housing laws. The United States Supreme Court refused to review the New Jersey Superior Court's decision. The upholding of the fair housing laws and the precedents established under them forecasts the legal future in this area of civil rights law.

The effect of the fair housing laws on the Negro population is also of considerable moment. The laws hold out the prospect of eventual freedom of movement. Because of the lag in Negro purchasing power, this mobility is still only a prospect even where anti-bias laws exist, but the morale of the minority group is nevertheless bolstered by the critical factor of motivation. The elite of the Negro population can become desegregated under such laws, giving a practical demonstration that it can be done, and the effect of these examples is exceedingly important in forstalling bitterness and giving hope for the future. The success of those who succeed in achieving mobility is magnified as it refracts through the Negro community.

Hence the effectiveness of fair housing practices laws seems assured.[8] Although they have not as yet produced substantial changes in the great Negro concentrations, their strategic function is great. Complemented by political forces, such laws will have a key role in what we hope will be a slow but steady exertion of public policy on behalf of fuller opportunity for Negroes. The educational activity of public Commissions on Human Relations will in time reach more and more people through the schools, the mass media and civic channels. In this latter respect, the trend is toward more constructive action on behalf of desegregation, rather than mere standing legal protections or simplified education. Through a co-ordination of the policies of government agencies in employment, planning, urban renewal and housing, a concerted attack on the practices sustaining segregation is gathering force.

Spearhead Groups

Another major phase of the movement to expand opportunities in housing is taking place outside the framework of government under private auspices. There are various spearhead

groups applying themselves to the specific job of arranging
housing leases and sales in defiance of prevailing racial restrictions. Some of these groups, such as the Minneapolis Interfaith
Fair Housing Program, sponsored by a number of local religious groups, aim simply at bringing willing buyers together
with willing sellers. The actual sales to Negro families under
the program have not been considerable, but the effect of the
program on local churches and the communities in general has
been noteworthy. The signing of open occupancy pledges by
members of white communities, as an adjunct to such a housing
introduction service, helps to soften up the opinion in restricted
areas.[9]

The most experienced and successful private group making
open occupancy sales of houses in a city-wide program is
Friends Suburban Housing, Inc., operating in the Philadelphia
metropolitan area, which we have already discussed in other
contexts.[10] Chartered as a real estate corporation, the organization hired real estate sales people and set about arranging
transactions between white suburbanites and qualified Negro
home buyers. The intention was to have members of the Society
of Friends and others sympathetic to desegregation assist in
trying to soften the impact of Negro entry into all-white communities in the restricted suburban perimeter of Philadelphia.
The community relations problems of the program at the local
level have been difficult because of a shortage of skilled personnel to carry out the time-consuming tasks of assuaging community resentment, but the actual property exchanges have grown
steadily. This has been due in no small part to the quiet, tireless
work of the Director of the organization, Margaret Collins.
Friends Suburban Housing has enabled some dozens of minority families to obtain modern suburban houses. In proportion to
the broad suburban expanses involved, the group's achievement
has been small. There have been disheartening rebuffs and frustrations. Local real estate offices have on many occasions

thwarted the transactions of Friends Suburban Housing. Within the Society of Friends there have been misgivings on the part of conservative elements. But the group has persisted. They arranged some of the sales to Negro families in Levittown, Pennsylvania, after the stormy entry into that community of the first Negro family.

Working with a full-time staff against all manner of opposition and difficulty, Friends Suburban Housing has shown what private initiative can do. In 1961 a subsidiary organization, Housing Investment Fund, Inc. (HIFI), was set up. This group is to serve as a conduit for funds to Friends Suburban Housing work, with the aim of enabling the group to acquire properties and hold them until suitable buyers are found—e.g., houses coming onto the market through sheriff's sales, mortgage foreclosures, the liquidation of estates, etc. Finding the right family for the right house is not easy. The number of Negro families resolute enough to enter the forbidden white neighborhoods is not so great that purchases can be casually arranged. Time is needed, and the use of HIFI to buy this time will be important. This will also make possible a larger interval for countering antagonistic opinion in the affected areas. Friends Suburban Housing has also sold houses to white families; the transactions that do not involve any abrogation of the racial code have provided funds to keep the organization moving. They also give practical demonstration that the group is not "for Negroes alone" but is truly committed to open occupancy.

Other such organizations are springing up in various cities. They are tender growths compared to the powerful real estate and building interests still committed to racial restriction. The religious motivation of those participating in these efforts is an important feature. It provides some assurance to the suspicious general white public that the groups are not aiming to exploit the issue of racial change. Combined with the influence of those mavericks in real estate and homebuilding, such as Modern Community Developers, which do not discriminate, their importance is growing. As has been noted before, it only takes one or a few Negro families to break down the ideal of the segregated local community. Add to these groups fostering Negro dispersion throughout the general market the random penetrations of single Negro families who defy segregation on their own initiative, and it becomes evident that the metropolitan real estate market will not in the future be able to conduct a comfortable "segregation as usual" business.

The active and constructive effort of Negroes to pierce restrictions in the housing market is still a specialized function carried on by liberal elite groups. Most Negro families are preoccupied with the older civil rights problems of employment and family educational deficiencies. Sooner or later, however, this pioneering movement is going to obtain the broad support of the multitudes of city Negroes. Then desegregation will proceed apace, and the most fundamental change in race relations since the great migrations from the South will take place.

Neighborhood Idealism

The historical dimensions of the racial problem dictate that the forthright opening of opportunities for residential mobility must be accompanied by a further process. As the foregoing chapters amply demonstrate, desegregation is a complicated movement, full of subtle difficulties. Responsible social leaders must be willing not only to set it in motion but to supervise and guide it. This brings us to the consideration of the community efforts to oversee and insure the success of racial readjustment in the urban community.

During the 1950's there were redoubtable efforts by public intergroup agencies and a wide variety of civic and neighborhood organizations to deal with racial change in a constructive manner. Much of this activity was a spontaneous response of sensible residents to wild rumors, real estate exploitation, and the panic psychology that often marked the first phase of nonwhite entry. The local groups often had a certain furious quality of moral idealism. They assaulted the problem with high hopes. The professional intergroup relations agencies, both public and private, were able to develop a whole series of program techniques for assisting the neighborhood stabilization groups. An impressive library of adult education and leadership training materials has been produced in connection with these local movements.[11]

There was also during the last decade a considerable research effort to establish the factual circumstances of racial change. Questions relating to migration, housing demand, real estate practices and price behavior in changing areas were subjected to competent economic and social-science scrutiny. The largest of these undertakings, that of the Commission on Race and Housing, resulted in five volumes which filled a great need for solid information about housing changes. The findings of such research were given publicity and digested in popular form for extensive distribution. Local public and private agencies studied the particular conditions in their areas. Such agencies as the New York Regional Plan Association, the Newark Commission of Human Relations, and the Philadelphia Commission on Human Relations produced valuable studies of local conditions. This research has certainly not answered all the major questions about racial change, but it has attacked the old half-truths and guesses about the subject with the keener tools of rational inquiry. It has enabled public officials and community leaders to deal more and more with the issues in realistic terms.

These developments during the 1950's were encouraging. They represented heartening citizen response to a difficult problem. To some extent the initial enthusiasm and democratic commitment were sustained, but in more cases this spirit wavered with time and was overcome by practical difficulties. This is part of the reason why segregation has sprung up in many formerly integrated areas. What were the flaws in this effort of urban civic leaders to meet the problem of racial change in housing? Did they not have law, factual data and good educational materials on their side? Why do they find themselves, at the beginning of the 1960's, looking ahead with trepidation?

Civic Casualties

If we view the community leadership and organization effort at the local level with a critical eye, certain things are evident. Local effort did much to reduce community tension, and the very fact that the attempt at local co-operative guidance was made is important. But various factors militated against their success. Owing to individualism and the mobility of urban life, the modern American city-dweller is strongly resistant to involvement in local organization or co-operative effort. When hasty attempts at co-operation are invested with all the emotional problems of the racial issue, the prospects are not very good. But the greatest weakness in this effort was probably lack of continuity. Volunteer leaders simply could not do all the work needed. Where full-time or even half-time staff was available, as in Hyde Park-Kenwood in Chicago or, prior to racial change, in Levittown, New Jersey, the results were notable.

Another factor was the failure of local institutions to co-operate fully in the movement. Churches, businesses and other institutions for the most part maintained a hands-off policy.

Some churches made great contributions, but these seemed to represent smaller denominations. The churches with long lines of communication and elaborate organization usually remained inert or aloof. Some of the larger universities joined the effort, not perhaps without regard to immediate self-interest. The pattern in the urban centers seems to have been one of institutions unable to overcome their inertia in the face of community change and disruption.

Even more serious than these defects, however, was the problem of failing morale among local leaders. There was almost a pattern to the growth of disillusionment, and this pattern was seldom related to objective facts in the neighborhood. Starting off with high ideals and a kind of romantic faith in their fellow men, the local leaders (who were usually not the ones with political experience) soon found the going hard. Certain typical defeats would be suffered. The secretary of the local group might get "nerves" and move out, mumbling about inter-racial marriage. Or one of the dozen Negro newcomers might have children who were no little Lord Fauntleroys. Down would go the morale. The neighborhood standards might be fine; the newcomers might on the whole be excellent neighbors; but a few typical set-backs would send the leaders to the wailing wall. Maybe this was because they were so class-conscious, or brittle, or inexperienced. Whatever the cause, sweet liberals turned sour in the process. I attribute the condition to the fact that the leaders were seldom prepared by long-term training to meet the inevitable tests of their convictions with calm determination. There just wasn't a strong enough will to win.

The research effort to provide reliable information about conditions surrounding racial change was valuable—as research. Unfortunately the work of making intelligible and popularizing the scholarly monographs and statistical monuments was not nearly extensive enough. The mass media were not utilized to the extent that certain basic established facts were put across to the man in the changing street with anything like the impact of cigarette commercials. Much of the research was national. Local agencies seldom had sufficient budget for an adequate study of local situations. Neighborhood people would reject out-of-hand conclusions about distant cities. They wanted to know about the here-and-now right in their own communities. These difficulties with research point up the fact that the popular mentality has often been contemptuous of any information which contradicted the store of traditional superstition about race.

The movement to secure and make effective fair housing legislation required immense labors on the part of civil rights groups and agencies; the legislative campaigns were usually long and exhausting. But for reasons we have already noted, when the legislation had been secured, complaints under the laws came in at a relative trickle. The direction of non-white housing demand was not perceptibly altered. Negro families continued to seek homes at the edge of the ghetto or in neighborhoods where there already was substantial integration. For all their significance as legal victories, long-range promises and important educational devices, fair housing laws had little initial effect on the rapidly consolidating segregation. This is not a reflection on the laws. It is a demonstration of the fact that the social prerequisites for non-white dispersion throughout the general housing market were simply not present.

Owing to such defects the neighborhood stabilization efforts of the 1950's have been inadequate to protect integrated communities against the forces that threaten them. Obviously the remedies for these defects would require a lengthy dissertation, and since my intention in this book is to review and analyze, rather than to suggest detailed programs, I will not indulge in any easy prescriptions.

Although newspapers have editorialized against real estate exploitation of racial change and against racial tension, it has been rare for the more powerful elements of the cities to come out in support of a stable integrated community. Perhaps conservative big-city leaders resent the population change too much to permit this. (The Greater Baltimore Committee is a notable exception, providing an example of top-level city interest in stabilization.) The banking fraternity, the big business network, the wielders of power on the urban scene have refrained from endorsing or in any way assisting integrated residential life. This will have to change if the social psychology which accepts segregation is to be broken down in the 1960's.

We must not only tie local organization to powerful organs of leadership opinion in the next ten years, but relate the areas working for racial harmony to actual programs of urban renewal, conservation and sources of housing demand if they are to survive. Too many of the integrated neighborhoods have gone down in splendid isolation under the tides of segregation. The question seems to be whether the entire urban community will see as its own problem the defense of stable interracial residential life.

One of the unresolved issues of policy for those dealing with this entire field is that of precisely defining their concept of ideal integration on the residential level. Attempts by Morton Gradzins (in *The Metropolitan Areas as a Racial Problem*) and Saul Alinsky (in 1959 testimony before the United States Civil Rights Commission) to interpret integration in numerical terms and recommend a proportional or percentage balance have led to outcries against "arbitrary quotas." The same criticism has been leveled at builder Morris Milgram of Modern Community Developers for his occupancy ratios in new developments. It is my belief that integration is a condition characterized by acceptance, security and civil relaxation with respect to race. This condition can be present within a wide range of numerical or proportional variations. It must, however, be founded on certain physical and psychological assurances in the local community, and the creating and fostering of these assurances is part of the job of leaders working with this problem. The quota issue boils down to a judgment of whether you can in fact have integration in our social situation without controls, whether you can in fact establish controls for many areas, and whether you value stable integration in housing so highly that you are willing to exclude some minority families and favor others in a community, purely to support the morale of whites.

The great debate about quotas should not blind us to the fact that there are many assurances other than guarantees against swift racial turnover that must be provided if residential integration is to be made possible for large areas. As a practical issue, the question of imposing housing quotas has not arisen often in the past, but it may in the future.

The 1960's will also provide the answer to the question of whether the suburbs will join the core cities in dealing with racial change. Places like New Rochelle, Deerfield and Levittown certainly share the problem, but the vast suburban perimeter is for the most part still exempt from trial. We can already state that unless this perimeter is tried by pioneering Negro families, the inner-city areas defending integrated conditions will be lost to the cause. They will become segregated by the pressure of non-white demand, particularly as the wartime crop of babies enters the marital age bracket. The answer to this question is held by the Negro families in the core city who have ambitions and a vague desire for the "next step" in the journey toward freedom from segregation. Their steps in the 1960's will have deep meaning for the future of our social life and for this history of our race relations.

It has been suggested by Marjorie Ware of Neighbors, Inc., in Washington, D.C., that a national conference of those working for the stabilization of integrated neighborhoods be held to re-examine the entire formula for this endeavor. This would be most helpful. An approach should be made to The American Council to Improve Our Neighborhoods for the sponsoring of such a conference. The businesslike conferences they have planned on other topics have been impressive. A gathering under such auspices could be kept from degenerating into an exchange of platitudes. Such a conference could chart the new strategy for integrated neighborhood activity in the 1960's.

The Professors

One of the most telling developments in the civil rights field has been the growth of practical involvement of educational and religious groups. The role of these elements in guiding and promoting racial change is bound to increase. The school desegregation furor of the 1950's placed educators squarely in the middle of the racial problem. The challenge to urban school systems in the North and West presented by the influx of culturally deprived Negro children has begotten a fresh perspective and some encouraging experiments to equalize educational opportunity.[12] Religious groups have also been subjected to changes that have required responses to racial movement. The religious growth of the 1950's brought an increase of membership and signs of greater maturity in the American religious outlook. The racial changes of the cities have forced a clarification of doctrine, policy and administration as one congregation after another faced Negro applicants and missionary work. The long-standing contradiction between what was preached and what was practiced has become starkly evident as racial change has begun to flow around the churches of the cities. These influences have aroused the educational and religious networks to try to make a positive contribution to the day-to-day process of mediating the great urban population shift.

Through the public and private school systems in the major cities adult education activities have been reshaped to include courses in human relations, race relations, community organization and leadership training. Social-science courses in race relations and ethnic problems have been developed. Institutes for human relations such as those at New York University and the University of Pennsylvania have trained police, teachers, social workers and intergroup relations personnel in the intricacies and techniques of racial problems. The educational institutions have also provided a reservoir of articulate leadership to staff speakers' bureaus, committees and study groups grappling with various phases of popular opinion or civic resistance.

The effect of this educational concentration is being felt in many areas of life. The formation of values and attitudes that begins at the primary school level is also working a change. Racial attitudes do improve with educational achievement.[13] In a time when the nation is keenly conscious of educational problems and the anti-intellectual aversion to academic leadership is on the wane, the role of urban institutions of learning can be highly effective. The prestige and leadership educational circles bring to racial problems bear great promise. There are difficulties that could immobilize the educators. Professional conservatism, the domination of trustees, or the tendency of private groups to exempt themselves from problems that involve the broader public could undercut educational concern. But in the urban areas where social life is inevitably so mixed, the educators must take part in what directly affects them. The seminars, study weeks, conferences and civic participation sponsored by educators are giving good evidence for the future that so far as they are concerned the issue is joined.

The principal question for the educators is not whether they will give intellectual leadership for desegregation, but how they will conduct the institutions in their care, especially the public schools. The public schools are frequently the key factor in the racially changing neighborhood. The white householders may grudgingly accept Negroes as neighbors but rebel against the prospect of sending their children to heavily Negro schools. Fears that Negro family problems may produce lack of motivation in Negro children affecting their school performance, and that the standards of the whole school will suffer, stir the resentment of white parents. Such parents withdraw their children from the mixed school.

The responses to such school withdrawals on the part of administrators have been inadequate. Very few school systems have any kind of positive program for stabilizing enrollment in the racially changing area. Measures for making the schools in such areas especially attractive are seldom devised. Curriculum enrichment, better staffs, more counselling, stronger parent-teacher groups and school boundary changes are rarely tried to offset the runaway mentality of white parents.[14]

If public school systems in the large cities have not worked successfully on the problem of the school in the changing area, the institutions of higher education have tended to be estranged from the minority populations surrounding them. Such institutions as Columbia, the University of Chicago and the University of Pennsylvania are in areas with encroaching non-white populations. Universities in such situations tend to worry about the effect on their enrollment and prestige of nearby minority neighborhoods with their low-income, problem families, etc. With redevelopment aid available, various large institutions are producing what amounts to a *cordon sanitaire* around themselves. These redeveloped university zones often squeeze out great numbers of Negro families of lower class and admit smaller numbers of upper-echelon Negroes into a rebuilt cap-and-gown area. The universities may use the crowded minority areas for social-science and medical surveys, but they seldom actively take these areas under their protection and campaign for them in partisan humanitarian fashion. The needs of the universities usually overcome altruism.[15]

The Preachers

Religious influence in the urban areas is difficult to assess. We are not a people who formally identify religion with our civic and public institutions. Individualism is so strong in urban society that the social influence of religious teaching is hard to determine. The American Protestant tradition was rooted in our rural past. Judaism and Catholicism were until recently the religions predominantly of immigrants. The novelty and power of industrial urban society was such that all religious groups were hard pressed to make their traditional evangelical approaches pertinent and respected. The major urban social institutions like the corporations, public schools, government and mass media can correctly be termed secular, since they lack religious origins and orientation and continue in this manner despite occasional deference to a vague pietism. Yet the sheer physical and organizational extent of religious congregations and their unmistakable vitality should indicate that the denominations are a potent social force in the urban areas. Their publications, educational works and interest in social trends and problems demonstrates the conscious commitment of the religious groups to the reform of urban society. Some groups lack a definite program, but others have specific aims

marshalled under the eye of a careful social criticism. If a slow-
ness of response has led many to conclude that religious groups
have lost concern for social issues, the lessons of history have
remained unread. There is a thoroughness to the conscious religious social apostolate that is slow in accumulating results
but profound in its ultimate effects.

For Protestantism the engagement with city racial problems
has been difficult. Widely varying Scriptural and doctrinal positions with respect to race led to confusion. In many cases the
independence of churches placed them beyond any real denominational guidance or assistance in confronting racial
change. Interdenominational co-operation is growing. The old
Scriptural rationalizations defending racial separation are
in disrepute among urban congregations and ministers. The
ties between all-Negro Baptist and Methodist churches and
their corresponding white denominational affiliates are increasing. The teaching about the moral basis of interracial justice
is becoming more consistent.

These changes in Protestantism are producing movements
under religious auspices which are energetically attacking racial problems. If there are churches which still reject Negroes
or move out of mixed neighborhoods, there are groups like the
pastoral mission collaborators in Harlem which aim to provide
religious and social assistance to the depressed Negro population. The teaching statements issued by Protestant groups have
become more specific in condemning housing segregation.[16] In
particular situations of racial change, ministers have worked
to uphold principles of Christian justice at great sacrifice.[17]

The Roman Catholic Church is heavily urban. Its roots in
this country are in the great cities where the immigrants hud-
dled together upon arriving from the Old World. It has had a
strong and consistent doctrinal teaching against segregation
and racial exclusion. It approached the racial problem in the

South through specialized missionary activity in the past. Unlike the Protestant churches of the South, it did not have large
numbers of adherents deeply enmeshed with the racial problem.
Today, however, the Catholic dioceses in the most populous
Catholic urban centers are invested with huge Negro concentrations. The Catholic institutions have a fair-to-good record
of accommodation to this Negro proximity. Their doors are
open and stay open, serving white and Negro alike. The mass
of Catholic parishioners may leave the neighborhood in prejudiced reaction, but the parish administration under priests,
nuns and some lay people remains to build the parish again
among the newcomers.[18]

Within the Catholic Church the pronouncements setting
forth tasks in interracial work have been made more explicit.
The 1958 statement of the bishops, "Discrimination and the
Christian Conscience," began a new era in the relationship of
the ancient church with the stubborn American racial problem. Following this statement Catholic Interracial Councils
increased rapidly. The National Catholic Conference for Interracial Justice was formed to guide work on a national scale. A
whole series of strategic statements on housing segregation were
issued, and Catholic support for fair housing legislation grew.
Priests have given well-publicized demonstrations of their interest in overcoming housing restrictions.[19]

Catholic leadership on behalf of housing desegregation can
be extremely important in the metropolitan centers. Most dioceses are metropolitan in geographical extent, including center city, suburbs and exurbs. This permits a breadth of view.
Because the cities have a heavy proportion of Catholics the
Catholic work for desegregation will have a broad impact in
them. The parishes, parochial school systems, colleges and
other institutions, adhering to their locations in the cities, will
be very influential social factors. Their traditions of inclusive-

ness and the prestige and supervised attention of their teaching will be a powerful solvent of segregation.

Jews are our most urban religious group. Their extraordinary educational and humanitarian achievements have greatly enriched the cities. (Their special problems with respect to racial change have been outlined in Chapter 5.) One thing is certain, and that is that the civil rights movement would be terribly maimed if Jews were not part of it. Whatever problems the Jewish communities have with desegregation, their leadership must remain committed to the ideal of social opportunity and full mobility. The minority tradition and consciousness within the Jewish group is enough to ensure this. The professional and front-line services the Jewish agencies have rendered in the desegregation struggle have created a strong liberal commitment. Jewish urbanites are so much part of the movement for desegregation that it is hard to think of the movement without their contribution.

The pervasiveness and social depth of religious influence in the city will more and more affect the segregation system in housing. The churches have an irrevocable claim to the right of forming the personal conscience. Their teachings penetrate to the family and to all those informal levels of association that defy legislation or formal organizational influence. Their unified action against segregation will probably provide the strongest challenge to racism yet made in our country's history if they abandon the tendency to rely solely on generalized preaching and bring their influence to bear on the situation more directly.

What has emerged in the governmental, civic and religious life of the cities is a hardy democratic brotherhood which is co-operating to oppose segregation, cynicism and community lethargy. The activity of the lawyers and local groups and religious leaders is a forecast of the order of tolerance that we

hope will prevail in our cities. The proponents of equal opportunity are sowing the wheat of social reform instead of the
cockle of racism. Whether or not the seed will grow depends
upon the winds of social change, the refreshing dews of idealism and the labors of the democratic citizenry.

NOTES

1. See M. Bamberger and N. Lewin, "The Right to Equal Treatment:
   Administrative Enforcement of Anti-Discrimination Legislation,"
   Harvard Law Review, January 1961, and "Racial Discrimination in
   Housing," *University of Pennsylvania Law Review,* February 1959.
2. Jack Greenberg, *Race Relations and American Law* (New York,
   Columbia University Press, 1959).
3. "Housing Bias Law Found Effective," *New York Times,* June 19,
   1960.
4. Dorsey vs. Stuyvesant Town Corp., 299 N.Y. 512, 87 NE 2d 541,
   1949.
5. Favors vs. Randall, 40 F. Supp. 743 (E.D. Pa. 1941).
6. State Commission Against Discrimination vs. Pelham Hall Apartments, 10 Misc. 2d, 334, 170 N.Y. S 2d. 250 (Sup. Ct. 1958). See
   also the California case of Ming vs. Horgan holding housing built
   with FHA guarantees to be "state aid." 3 Race. Rel. L. Rev. 693
   (1958) Calif. Super. Ct.
7. Levitt and Sons vs. D.A.D. 56 N. J. Super. 542 (1959).
8. See *New York Times,* June 19, 1960, art. cit. Typical of a dissent
   from the use of fair housing laws are the views of J. S. Purnell of T.
   Mellon and Sons at the 50th Conference of the National Urban
   League in which this banker expresses strong reservations about
   such laws.
9. See "The Housing Introduction Service" published by the Omaha
   Urban League.
10. The story of Friends Suburban Housing is summarized by H. H.
    Dexter in *What's Right with Race Relations* (New York, Harper,
    1958), p. 92.
11. The activities of some of the typical neighborhood groups are de-
    scribed in Hannah Lees, "Negro Neighbors," *The Atlantic Monthly,*

January 1956, and A. Nicholson and E. Rosen, "When a Negro Moves Next Door," *The Saturday Evening Post,* April 4, 1959.

12. The experiments in enriching public schools programs in New York's P. S. 40 have gained wide attention. The Washington, D.C., and St. Louis education efforts have also been widely discussed. See Carl F. Hansen, "A Five-Year Report on Desegregation in Washington, D.C, Schools" in *Southern School News,* April 1960.

13. A Study by the Connecticut Commission on Civil Rights in April 1960 showed that those most likely to accept Negro neighbors were college graduates, those least likely had not finished grammar school.

14. An excellent program was devised by the Wilmington, Delaware, public schools and the National Conference of Christians and Jews. See Delaware Chapter, National Conference of Christians and Jews, *An Adventure in Human Relations—A Three-Year Report on Schools in Changing Neighborhoods.*

15. A major exception to this ivory-tower complex has been in the provision of medical aid and services. University medical centers have been of great benefit to slum areas. But off-campus faculties and academic withdrawal from the works of local community service have deprived minority areas of needed direction. True, the notable Chicago University school of urban sociology has done much to enlighten us intellectually on slum problems, but this is different from providing leadership and resources for reconstruction of local life. Recently a change has been taking place as urban renewal has put one campus after another into the scheme of urban rebuilding.

16. See T. B. Maston, *Segregation and Desegregation* (New York, Macmillan, 1959); The National Council of Churches of Christ, *The Churches' Concern for Housing;* The United Church of Christ, *Housing without Racial Barriers* (November 1957); The Presbyterian Church, U.S.A., "Residential Desegregation" in *Social Progress,* September 1958.

17. The inspiring work of the Reverend Daniel Stevick in Levittown, Pennsylvania, is described in the proceedings of the 1959 Conference of the National Association of Intergroup Relations Officials. A Methodist minister in Garden Grove, California, displayed wise Christian leadership similar to that of many other local clergymen. See "Racism in Suburbia" in *The Christian Century,* April 10, 1957.

18. The Roman Catholic officials of New York, Chicago, Washington, D.C., and Boston and Worcester, Massachusetts, all have active programs to aid parishes in older neighborhoods and continue parish work amid population and urban renewal changes.

19. Cardinal Albert Meyer of Chicago gave a strong statement before the U. S. Civil Rights Commission in 1960 about discrimination in housing. The National Catholic Conference for Interracial Justice set forth a clear position in a statement issued in 1960. Catholic spokesmen supported fair housing laws in New York, Pennsylvania, Connecticut, Minnesota and Rhode Island. See issues of *Trends,* 1959, 1960, 1961. Individual priests and laymen have worked for racial justice in housing in various areas. See the *Interracial Review,* published by the Catholic Interracial Council, New York.

9

The Determinants of Change

To TRY to summarize the different influences at work among urban racial concentrations, we must now draw the various factors into some ordered form. The segregation influences discussed thus far are complex and interacting. There are conditions pertaining to racial change that we have not explored in full. In a book of this kind it would be impossible to do so. The material presented here is largely of a survey nature, for extensive technical analysis would have to be the subject of a large and formidable work. In order to interrelate the broad themes of the foregoing chapters, we shall now set forth a tentative hypothesis with regard to the determinants of urban racial movement. This hypothesis is not presented as in any sense a complete framework of social thought fully explaining nonwhite mobility and concentration. Its utility is that it permits a restatement of a variety of factors in a somewhat more concentrated and coherent form.

For purposes of exposition we could state our hypothesis as follows: The major factors determining the concentration and the direction of non-white residential movement in major urban centers have been:

1. Non-white population growth.
2. The limitations of non-white income.

3. The location of existing non-white concentrations.

4. The disposition of neighborhoods toward non-white entry because of fluid social and economic conditions.

5. Neighborhood cults of ethnic solidarity and racial exclusion.

6. Physical obstacles that act as social barriers.

7. Real estate manipulation of property acquisition to restrict and direct non-white movement.

The factors enumerated in this listing are not ranked according to importance. Such a ranking would be impossible, owing to vast differences in local conditions and residential patterns which have resulted in the prominence of one or another factor according to the trends in a given time or place. On the whole, however, urban racial change has involved the interplay of all of these factors within the residential life of the major cities.

Population Growth

Residential expansion of the non-white populations in the urban areas has corresponded with periods of population growth. In the nineteenth century, the importation of Negroes from Southern communities to work on railroads and other projects expanded the minority concentrations. In the cities of Washington, Baltimore and Philadelphia, in-migration frequently caused changes in the shape of the Negro areas. Even such events as the migration caused by the race riots in Wilmington, North Carolina, in 1890 and in Atlanta, Georgia, in 1906 produced alterations in the Negro neighborhoods in Northern cities. During World War I the demand for Negro labor in Northern shipyards and factories brought about the greatest alteration of racial boundaries after the Civil War period. World War II had a similar, and an even more far-reaching, effect. Labor migrations to Detroit, Chicago and Philadelphia swiftly expanded the ghettos in these cities.

Just as important as in-migration was the steady population growth of the non-white Negro concentrations due to native-born natural increase. The non-white birth rate per thousand women of childbearing age in most of the large cities was almost twice the rate for the whites in those cities. This disparity cannot be applied to the general population, however, for increases in the white population were concentrated in the suburban areas inhabited by the younger white families in post-war years. Thus within the boundaries of the old cities the non-white increase seemed even more extraordinary than it was, because the comparable white phenomenon of family increase was taking place outside the old city limits. The movement of non-white families beyond the limits of the traditional segregated areas after World War II was the first large-scale racial change that crossed class lines in the urban areas. Racial change had previously been almost entirely on the working-class level, but now to a great extent middle- and upper-class neighborhoods were affected in the major cities.[1]

Times of great population growth—usually times of crisis or periods of prosperity—are ordinarily accompanied by a loosening of the traditional social structure and customs. In a highly technical industrial society population growth is complex and extensive, so that social changes occur at many levels of community life. Such periods promote a reorganization of the segregation system as well as the extension of it. The growth of non-white population provides both the necessity and the impetus for the redistribution of the housing supply. This growth, however, has not been so decisive or critical as to shatter the deep-rooted controls of the residential segregation system.

Limitations of Income

The limited buying power of the Negro in the housing market supplemented the social pressures restricting mobility. The money to purchase mobility just did not exist for most Negroes. Even in the 1950's Louis Winnick was writing that ". . . the weight of present evidence seems to be that low income is a more strategic factor in the unfavorable density standards (i.e. crowding) of non-whites than housing discrimination per se."[2]

The inability to buy adequate housing led to overcrowding and confinement in the slum areas where housing was cheap in relation to costs in the rest of the housing supply. The fact that the cost of housing was dear in relation to the net income of Negro families and in relation to the meager amount of space purchased merely added to the distress.

This handicap helped to establish the assumption in the real estate market and in popular opinion that non-white accommodations had to be co-extensive with the least desirable locations. It also conditioned a great number of Negro families to downgrade their housing preference and set their expectations at a lower level. Such families, who read the minority press and other limited media, were for many years passed over by the sales efforts of the real estate industry. Even today Negroes are not the targets of the full blast of housing and other advertising. The limitations of Negro income curtailed the ambition and the ability to look for housing outside the ghetto. It is, for example, very difficult to hunt for a house in outlying areas and suburbs without an automobile. These facts have been decisive in establishing an immense inertia with respect to residential desegregation in the large urban Negro communities.

The first major changes in the shape of the Negro concentrations in the urban centers in decades occurred during the

1920's, when there was a period of high prosperity. The next series of major shifts occurred during the 1940's and the 1950's. These changes represented an uncoiling of Negro demand in the market, but under controlled conditions. During the 1950's it was still true that non-white income was on the average only half that of whites.[3] The rate of unemployment among Negroes during the economic recession periods in the 1950's and early 1960's was double that of whites. The buying power of Negroes was still subject to a multitude of special perils.

Low income has in the past confined Negroes to those neighborhoods in which poorer housing was available, and this has meant areas of old or even obsolete housing and areas where environmental factors have made the housing less desirable. "Negro residence" and "slum" were for years almost synonymous. Negroes lived in the "bottoms," "beside the tracks," or in "back streets." This has begun to change in recent years, but it still is the major pattern. Now that urban renewal has arrived, these substandard areas are receiving attention, albeit in piecemeal fashion. Renewal has reshaped the Negro concentrations to some extent. The access of Negro families to public low-rent projects has extended non-white residence in some cases outside the boundaries of the traditional Negro areas as these families occupied projects in previously vacant or all-white areas.

The income factor has not only been one of the chief determinants of the racial residential pattern; it has also acted to guarantee and preserve this pattern in the face of desegregation trends through the perpetuation of the poor credit standing of Negroes and the rejection of Negroes as a potential market for first-class housing.

Non-White Concentrations

The movement of Negroes has been related very closely to the proximity of concentrations of non-white population. The Negro areas have seldom grown by dramatic detachment of "colonies" of non-whites which ventured far beyond the segregated districts to establish substantial new islands of non-white residence, although there has been a little leapfrog movement that carried families far out beyond the rim of the Negro neighborhoods. The changes in racial distribution in residential life have usually resulted from expansion at the edge of the segregated areas.[4] This expansion has been brought about by the steady entry of non-whites into areas that were newly "broken" and made available for Negro occupancy. Depending upon the local conditions and the interpretation of the housing exchange, the expansion process can be described either as a displacement of whites in areas adjacent to the ghetto or as the filling of a real estate vacuum by Negroes.

The ability to see, inspect and move to distant dwellings has been retarded. Hence houses within walking distance of their present residence are the most accessible to Negro families. The institutions that serve the needs of the minority group in an uncongenial society may be highly valued by Negroes, who would tend to stay close to the segregated area, where the full choice of such institutions would be available. In a low-income group the informal associations surrounding family and residential life are important as alternatives to formal organizations. The traditions of affinity and of "folk fellowship" in the segregated areas have a magnetic influence that holds great numbers of Negro families in relatively close relationships with the ghetto.

Psychologically, the ghetto acts as an emotional and mental backstop for the Negro family that attempts to enter an all-white block for the first time. There is reassurance in knowing that other Negroes are only one block or four blocks away. The nearby ghetto is a refuge giving a promise of aid and sympathy if needed and an opportunity for social contact without the uncertainties and intimidations of the prejudiced world "outside." [5]

There are business reasons why the Negro population has spread by moving directly to adjacent areas in the major cities. Real estate brokers could specialize in Negro clientele and be sure of a steady supply of Negro customers if they operated close to the ghetto. They could also control the change better at this range, for the perimeter of the ghetto was usually a taut market in the sense that alertness and strong pressures prevailed in this zone. White residents could usually foresee the approach of racial change, and the assumption was mechanical that once a block was entered by Negroes, no real estate broker would sell to anybody but Negroes. In areas farther removed from the Negro population, racial entry, on the rare occasions when it occurred, was likely to be attended by far greater excitements. The cynical controls and assumptions were not clearly established for such areas. But close to the edge of the ghetto, a sort of grim segregationist logic governed racial change. The forces of increased Negro demand, slackened white demand, environmental changes, chance penetrations, etc., were manipulated according to a set of rules which governed the advance of Negro occupancy, setting its limits according to market factors, arbitrary whims or physical demarcations.

Fluid Conditions

When the social or economic character of a neighborhood is altered in a fundamental manner, the possibility of non-white entry and racial change is increased. This is, of course, particularly true of neighborhoods close to the non-white concentrations. Changes in the local social structure, institutions or property pattern require readjustments in neighborhood life. These changes may cause population shifts.[6] The traditional controls and real estate practices may pass into new hands. Leadership and local morale and opinion may change. What begins as an alteration of the white population within the framework of a racially restricted housing market may provide the opportunity for non-whites to acquire property in the area. The conditions causing such housing turnover frequently interlock, so that the causes are seldom independent.

An enumeration of some of the common social changes that can dispose neighborhoods to non-white entry will make clear how these factors operate.

1.   Changes in environmental factors can lead to population turnover in an area, and the resulting heavy exchange of property can permit more opportunity for Negro entry. The encroachment of offensive industrial and commercial property uses may lead long-time residents to move. Slaughterhouses, all-night service industries, new highways, etc., may represent blighting influences to white residents. At times the consignment to Negroes of houses near such influences is rather readily conceded, once the undesirability of the location has become clear. In other areas the exodus of some factory or institution can be the occasion for white families to migrate.

2.   Changes in property tenure can trigger racial change. When owner occupancy patterns begin to dissolve in favor of a property tenure pattern of absentee ownership, renting, subleasing and transient occupancy, the agreement about racial exclusion can be undermined. The need for tenants may lead some property owners to rent to non-whites. The growth of rentals may also lead to an increase in the density of the area.

3.   Obsolescent properties that are no longer attractive to

white buyers or renters may be opened to Negroes, whose more limited housing choice often makes such properties comparatively attractive. Dwellings with outmoded facilities, high maintenance costs or deteriorated appointments have been conveniently shifted to the Negro market in many cities.

4. Changes in housing preference have many times led to the abandonment of neighborhoods by great numbers of white families. The preference of families for suburban living, increases in the family, the desire for more modern housing in terms of design and new appliances have all caused movement out of older neighborhoods. Sometimes the affinity of ethnic groups plays a role in the evacuation of families from neighborhoods. Italian-Americans and Polish-Americans may move to newer settlements in an informal but definitely concerted fashion. Such changes can lead to the replacement of the original groups by non-whites.

5. The existence of high vacancy rates due to economic recessions and unemployment can make properties available to Negroes. Times of prosperity may promote large-scale housing exchange as families seek to improve their housing conditions, and they may leave a vacuum of unoccupied properties in an area. Real estate dealers may feel compelled to fill this vacuum by selling or leasing to Negro prospects.

6. Speculation on the part of real estate dealers can be decisive in promoting racial turnover. White real estate brokers may be unable to resist the large number of commissions to be made on housing sales if racial panic among the residents of an area can be induced. Negro real estate brokers may genuinely feel that they are advancing the improvement of non-white housing by participating in the speculative turnover of a neighborhood.

7. A high rate of mobility of the occupants of a neighborhood may lessen the controls upon occupancy and result in

non-white entry. The rapid turnover of families due to wartime movement and pressing industrial labor needs resulted in a relaxation of racial restrictions in urban areas in some sections of the country. In some places wartime housing projects placed Negroes in white neighborhoods for the first time.

8. Changes in the families characteristic of a neighborhood can, in turn, alter its property-tenure pattern. Houses occupied by large families that move out may be converted to rooming-house use and eventually to Negro occupancy. Neighborhoods built and occupied at one period by families of similar age may at a later date be held by these families, when they are an aging group, as rental property. This may result in a number of properties coming onto the market simultaneously, as the elderly families die or relinquish the properties that have become a burden to them in later years.

9. Changes in neighborhood morale can lead to racial change. The dissolution of neighborhood consensus and mutual confidence can bring about racial change through spite sales. A decline of neighborhood morale may lead to the deterioration of property until the property becomes unattractive to white owners or renters.

10. Periods of housing shortage may so increase the competition for housing that minority families may seek dwellings in defiance of racial restrictions. The housing shortage may be in the general housing market or it may apply only to the non-white community. Such shortages can lead to racial changes that are exploitive of both the white families displaced and the Negro newcomers.

Cults of Exclusion

The concentration of white immigrant groups in certain areas of the cities has created pockets and zones of strong resistance to racial change. Feelings of ethnic affinity and rejection of "out groups" have, as has been explained in Chapter 5, erected racial barriers. The influences of these urban ethnic concentrations has not always been one of resistance, however. Jews, and some Puerto Rican and Portuguese groupings, may actually provide more tolerant affiliations for Negroes than the general white community. Such tolerance can lead to the sharing of a residential area. Hence the proximity of such immigrant groups to the Negro residential areas has helped to shape the ghetto, here resisting, there dissolving to permit, Negro succession. In some localities the tradition of anti-Negro vigilance established by an ethnic group may persist long after that group has lost numerical significance. The neighborhood cult of racial exclusion may be taken up and maintained by other white residents who eventually occupy the area.

It could be argued that racial reactions vary with the social and economic level of the neighborhood. Upper-class neighborhoods frequently respond to the prospect of Negro entry with a variety of legal and social pressures typical of the business and professional world in which the urban elite functions. Attempts may be made to "buy the Negro out," or bribe him, to frustrate change. Middle-class areas often respond by holding protest meetings and signing petitions—tactics typical of the civic-minded middle class. Areas occupied by semi-skilled and unskilled workers many times respond with simple rude intimidation or violence. These reactions spring out of the inability of the lower social and economic group to muster alternative expressions of resentment against racial change.[7]

The revival of interest in community organization in the 1950's raises the possibility that neighborhood organizations with paid staff, clear boundaries and access to urban renewal and rehabilitation programs may become commonplace in the cities. Such organizations can be formidable if they are committed to racial exclusion.[8] They could cast the local fear of racial change into businesslike form and capitalize on this fear for years.

In areas close to Negro concentrations, opinions about racial exclusion are often explicit, as has been noted previously in this chapter. As the distance from the Negro areas increases, the "watchdog" mentality usually abates. In the outlying areas of the city some traditional pockets of Negro residence may even be tolerated, as long as there is little chance of their expanding. In the suburbs the sentiment against racial change is normally vague, with an "it can't happen here" quality. Thus the advent of Negroes as residents tends to have maximum shock effect.

Whatever the location of the racially restricted neighborhood, the native white inhabitants commonly have some historical lore about how minority families have been rejected when they sought to enter or when they "stepped out of bounds."

Physical Barriers that Serve as Social Brakes against Mobility of Racial Groups

Industrial belts, railroad lines, expressways, rivers, parks and traffic arteries have been convenient physical obstacles to non-white movement, serving to cordon off non-white areas. At times the influence of such barriers has been great, freezing the racial pattern along a certain geographical line for decades. The redevelopment activity in the urban areas and the changes in commercial, industrial and residential life give evidence that many traditional physical barriers will be moved as the city landscape alters. There is today unquestionably more ability on the part of non-white families to surmount these barriers in their housing choices. We can expect, however, that such physical factors will continue to play a role in demarcating non-white residential areas.

Real Estate Manipulation

While the new housing supply is commonly closed to Negroes, the used-house market is manipulated according to the racial preferences and attitudes of real estate brokers, mortgage brokers, government housing personnel and the white residential population.[9] The effect of such manipulation upon non-white occupancy has been discussed at some length in Chapter 4. Despite the growth of fair housing practices legislation and the promise of diversification in non-white housing acquisitions, there is little prospect that there will be a relaxation of business practices preventing full mobility for minority families.

The foregoing factors have in the past been the determinants of racial change in the large urban areas. Separately and in concert they have militated against free movement of non-whites and determined the shape of racial concentrations. These factors represent a complex of economic, sociological and intellectual factors. In the South, and in other areas before the Supreme Court's 1948 decision rendering the restrictive covenants on property useless, these determinants have been supplemented by the law in their restrictive operation.

It does not require any special insight to understand that all seven of these determinants are still very much with us in the large cities. They are not as uniformly effective as they once were, but they are still the basic factors frustrating housing choice by the non-white group.

But there are new currents in the stream of urban life, which are giving a new impetus to racial movements. These new influences are threefold. First there is the growing pressure for equality of opportunity in housing. The heightened morale and social status of non-white families has engendered new housing demands. The fair housing practices laws act as levers with which the elite of the Negro population will gradually pry up local restrictions. The pressure for broader housing opportunity is largely a development of public opinion. Non-white opinion is becoming clearer in its housing demands, and white opinion is becoming less certain and intransigent in its restrictions. The whole trend of social life in the cities toward greater mobility and advancement in the standard of living defies the restrictive codes based upon race and tends to erode the factors that have previously determined racial settlement.

Second, changes in income have dramatically placed the Negro in a competitive position in portions of the housing market that were previously inaccessible. The numerical size of the Negro middle class that is striving for full choice in housing is not nearly as important as its strategic significance. The financially competent Negro family is not only a sound business risk for a housing transaction; it is a symbol, a forerunner, a promise of a bigger, untapped market for housing in the non-white group. The importance of this development for American race relations can hardly be overstated.

Finally, within the Negro group there is underway a change in housing preferences.[10] Urban living, mass communications and advertising are raising the expectations and housing tastes of the non-white population generally. The white population in the last twenty years has itself undergone a great transformation of housing tastes. The suburban image and the streamlined, horizontal house have attracted thousands. We can expect that non-whites will be increasingly attracted too by a similar set of preferences. It is possible that a different, more "downtown" set of fashions and values will intervene to shape the growing non-white demand for housing improvement.

This triad of influences gives grounds for optimism.[11] It serves to offset somewhat the weighty negative factors enumerated in the early part of this chapter. True, the seven long-standing traditional factors have inertia on their side. The new developments, however, have the dynamic and unpredictable power of current social change in their favor.

Whether or not a hypothesis such as that set forth in these pages is fully credible and explanatory, the need for such a conceptual framework is patent. Our major cities are facing massive racial changes without any adequate understanding of the forces directing these changes. An examination of the past racial movement in the cities would be helpful. Racial change has been such a controversial subject, so bedevilled with cynical, sinister and prejudiced interpretations, that we have not studied it comprehensively and objectively. Many studies have been undertaken solely for the purpose of refuting some popular prejudice. A more objective and broader outlook is needed. Studies of urban property history, ethnic succession, census comparisons and community changes are badly needed.[12]

At the present time the works produced by the Commission on Race and Housing and the New York Regional Plan Association are the outstanding contributions to our knowledge of the racial changes of the urban population. These studies are not specific enough to give local officials a true understanding of the problems of their cities. Each city has manifold characteristics and a history distinctly its own. The Commissions on Human Relations and intergroup relations agencies in the cities are seldom set up to do more than minimal research. The budgets are comparatively low and the research of such agencies looks more to immediate problems than to the history of change and future trends.

While it is true that analysis of racial change may not yield any reliable criteria that can be used to forecast non-white movement, we must know what forces are influencing such movement if we are realistically to continue working for increased housing opportunity and stable interracial community life. The cities are becoming more and more committed, morally, legally and socially, to such aims. They need, therefore, accurate knowledge of racial concentration, expansion and dispersion if they are to help adjust their community life to these racial changes in a responsible fashion.[13]

Perhaps the City Planning Commissions of the cities should be charged with analyzing racial change. Heretofore the planners have been shy of this task for understandable reasons. The embattled planners were hard pressed to establish prestige and some defenses of order, rational physical change and urban renewal. The physical planning programs left little time for consideration of the processes of population change. It would be a logical part of comprehensive planning to do something more than tabulate and statistically project population figures.

NOTES

1. The 75th Anniversary Booklet of the Philadelphia Tribune newspaper notes such changes.
2. Glazer and McEntire, *Studies in Housing and Minority Groups,* ch. vii.; Research Department of the Welfare Council of Metropolitan Chicago, Statistics, November and December, 1956; The Philadelphia Commission on Human Relations, *Non-White Residential Patterns* (June 1959).
3. B. Duncan and P. Hauser, *Housing a Metropolis—Chicago* (Glencoe, Ill., The Free Press, 1960). This excellent study affirms much of the comment in this chapter about non-white income, housing conditions, preferences and market behavior. See ch. 6, "Non-White Differentials in Housing."
4. L. Winnick, *American Housing and Its Use* (New York, Wiley, 1957), p. 69.
5. E. Ginsberg, *The Negro Potential* (New York, Columbia University Press, 1957), p. 16.
6. L. Laurenti, *Property Values and Race* (Berkeley, University of California Press, 1960). In Laurenti's test areas in San Francisco and Oakland the first racial changes came about through leapfrog

movement in most cases. In other cases there were moderate-sized Negro or mixed areas nearby. The areas chosen for study were largely those removed from the edge of heavy non-white concentrations. If we look at the maps of Negro residence and census data for major cities, however, it is indisputable that most racial turnover in housing has been at the ghetto's edge, with dispersions more distant than one or two miles, such as those in Laurenti's study, of lesser significance in terms of satisfaction of the housing requirements of Negro families. See Donald O. Cowgill, "Trends in Residential Segregation of Non-Whites in American Cities, 1940-1950," *American Sociological Review*, November 21, 1956.

7. H. Ashmore, *The Other Side of the Jordan* (New York, Norton, 1960). Ashmore quotes Lester Granger of the Urban League as saying, "People want to and probably need to stay among their own kind when they are strangers trying to make a new life in unfamiliar surroundings" (p. 110).

8. Attention was drawn to the role of such conditions in promoting ethnic change by the studies of Bessie McClenahan. See "Social Causes of Decline of Neighborhoods," *Social Forces*, May 1942. Mobile areas are characterized by "limited purpose" housing suitable for people in unstable life stages. See P. Rossi, *Why Families Move* (Glencoe, Ill., The Free Press, 1956).

9. Dennis Clark, "Racial Change in Three Kinds of Neighborhoods," *Journal of the National Association of Intergroup Relations Officials*, July 1958.

10. The organizations in Grosse Point, Michigan, and Deerfield, Illinois, have been cited before in these pages. See *Hearings of the U. S. Civil Rights Commission, 1960*.

11. L. Laurenti, *op. cit.*, cites the case of the Columbia Gardens area in Oakland, California, where racial change followed rapidly in the wake of the decision by white real estate brokers and leaders to start selling to Negroes. The intricacy of property restrictions and transactions can strangle desegregation. See G. Nesbitt, "Misconceptions of the Movement for Civil Rights in Housing," *Journal of the National Association of Intergroup Relations Officials*, Winter 1960-1961.

12. R. Weaver, "The Changing Status of Racial Groups," *Journal of the National Association of Intergroup Relations Officials*, Winter 1960-1961.

13. Foote *et al.*, *Housing Choices and Constraints*. The authors of this very notable book point out that what has been hailed as non-white housing improvement in recent years may not necessarily be advantageous. Non-white purchases have been in older areas or slums, and ". . . the Negro, of whatever income group, is still typically consigned to the oldest and least desirable sections of the city" (p. 128).

10

Formula for Urban Freedom

WHAT IS TO BE the future of the desegregation movement in housing? Will its leadership lose energy and settle down to a large-scale withdrawal from the arena of race relations in the urban areas? This could happen. The professional and civic leaders in civil rights, never particularly united, might bog down in a welter of law enforcement and technical squabbles. Erratic and extremist groups, like the Black Muslims, could grow and add to the confusion.[1] The Negro populations could elect to raise the level of their housing supply within the ghetto through urban renewal and avoid the vexations of desegregation. The recalcitrant white population could settle back into a prolonged period of social reserve, defending the bastions of suburbia with occasional sallies of segregationist propaganda. These things are all possible.

The urban leadership concerned with housing desegregation is at a puzzling stage in its campaign. The logic of the campaign is conclusive. Even if they concede the validity of voluntary racial concentrations as wholesome social groupings, they must still promote that equality of opportunity which is the dynamic of our economic and social life. Yet the movement to expand this opportunity has been slow and full of exasperations, even where the law has been an instrument of change. The work of guiding racial change, moderating tension and stabilizing racially mixed areas has met with numerous setbacks. The segregation process has usually maintained its old power of running its course and terminating in total racial turnover in residential life. The exceptions to these trends have demonstrated that an alternative of harmonious, desegregated local life is possible and workable in every way, given reasonable conditions.

What we can look forward to is a continuation of the trends promoting social and geographical mobility. The economic drawbacks of segregation will become more and more clear. The national interest in utilizing the potential of the minority population will emphasize the economic waste of segregation. The economic breaching of segregation has inevitable results of mobility. The buying power of Negroes will be ever more eloquent testimony against housing restrictions. If we add the increasing social acceptance of housing desegregation to the trends of economic improvement and mobility, we can see the erosion of the dikes of social custom and opinion that have supported segregation. Poverty, limited mobility and hostility are all passing as influences sustaining segregation.

The residential segregation of the past was maintained as part of a patchwork of urban ethnic partition. It was sanctioned by a legacy of superstition and ignorance that is now being dissipated. The civic climate of urban life is becoming less congenial to racial separation because of educational advances and a greater homogeneity of the urban population. The awareness of democratic commitments on the part of the general public, the ability of strategic pressure groups to command government sympathy for civil rights, and the hard fact of the legal definition of fair practices have changed the entire urban outlook. The urban population today is capable of a much more thorough self-examination with respect to racial restrictions than in the past. The moral, legal and cultural foundation of racial separation has been fissured in dozens of ways. The specious interpretations of Scripture which found segregation enjoined by the Bible, once so potent in a rural Protestant society, are now discredited in a religiously plural and partly secularized society. The legal covenants restricting sale of property are void, and laws now affirmatively prevent the use of race as a consideration in economic and property exchange. Public opinion increasingly recoils from the exposure of racial injustices in an era of sensitive international competition.

Past Failure

Granting all these changes, we cannot escape the fact that we have permitted the imposition of racial segregation in our major cities on a vast scale. Literally millions of Negroes are enmeshed in the complexities of the racially restrictive residential system. We have gambled with racism. We have bided our time as a nation, postponing this problem while we gave our attention to more pleasant undertakings like the building of suburbia, the expansion of the pleasure-boat industry and the development of greater mass media channels. True, the sundering of the racist tradition would have required heroic efforts. The reward would have been to free our nation of a shackle that has crippled it since birth. We made the choice in the hectic wartime and post-war years. These years were times of change, when the impetus of social reorganization would have aided us. They were years of patriotic feeling when we could have capitalized on a sense of national unity and purpose. We are now confronted with segregated residential life on such a large scale that there may be little we can do but hope that the active forces of our society will continue to work in behalf of the national interest by subjecting the urban racial concentrations to their attrition. But the twisted stubbornness of the racial problem in the past should sober us in any reliance upon such a course. The segregation tradition endows it with special potential for survival.

Harry Ashmore has written: "No one, then, has reason to assume that the segregated Negro bastions of the great cities will disappear any time soon—although in every one of them internal improvement of environment and services is a matter of urgent public business." [2] An analysis of the public housing and urban renewal programs in the cities by one critic concludes that the portions of the Negro urban population most in need of improvement have been passed over. David Carlson, in his articles, contends that the social adjustment of the increased Negro population to the urban environment has been poor and that the government renewal programs have been too small and too narrowly conceived to be of widespread value. He sees the prospects for desegregation as rather dim.[3] In actual terms of population distribution, the last ten years have not been encouraging. While there have been slight increases in the number of Negroes in suburban localities in New York, the picture for the rest of the nation is far less hopeful.[4] In 1961 the American Population Association was told that the suburbs of twelve major cities studied had remained 93% white over a thirty-year period. In five of the twelve areas the ratio of non-whites to the white population in suburbia actually declined.[5]

Seymour Lipset contends that the "development of both the theory and the practice of 'equalitarianism' among the white majority (in industrial society) has been aided by the continued presence of large, ethnically segregated castes." [6] The majority elements of our society, says Lipset, could sustain strong belief in our system of opportunities because "a disproportionate share of poverty, unemployment, sickness and all forms of deprivation have fallen to the lot of minority groups, especially fifteen million Negro Americans." [7] If such an estimate is true, then the power elements of urban society may still need segregation to polarize the deleterious social effects inherent in their system. Louis Wirth pointed out that ghettos have been traditionally established by an "unwitting crystallization" rather than by arbitrary authority.[8] Today, however, because of the growth of the state and the organizations of social control, segregation must be underwritten and ratified by explicit or implicit government consent. The extensiveness of state decisions assures that segregation in the future will have to be endorsed by government authority if it is to be maintained.

The possibility of a government benediction on residential segregation in the future raises the possibility of the most sinister kinds of temptation. If the state fair housing practices laws prove to result more in legal tangles of frustration than in rapid housing improvement, the reaction in government circles is likely to be a sense of defeat. Nor should we underestimate the cynical casuistry of urban society. It is not difficult to conceive of political and social leadership which, while manipulating a noisy display of legal and rhetorical devices in ostensible support of desegregation, set itself privately for segregation. We have seen this crafty game played with persistent success in the past. The drawback to such machinations today is that they cannot be acted out on a solid stage of social inertia before a largely apathetic minority audience. New abilities and resources in the minority population make the game of two-faced hypocrisy on racial matters much less practicable. The very affluence, mobility and freedom of communications in the sophisticated cities have brought the racial problem to a head.

Indeed the atmosphere of the cities can be said to have produced the present dilemma and endowed it with an imperative logic of tension and conflict.[9]

The extent of housing improvement for non-whites, the extent of desegregation and the kind of climate in which racial change takes place are all, then, in the hands of the leaders of urban society. The basic social forces are in motion to induce change. The urban leaders must determine how well or how badly these forces are guided and used to strengthen democratic society.

New Caesars

The various business and civic cadres in the urban areas have been discussed at different points in the foregoing chapters. There is considerable evidence that the economic and political leaders of the major cities are becoming realistically engaged with the question of housing desegregation. The spectacle of the central ghettos with their combination of progress in redevelopment and severe welfare problems has not only alarmed the liberal do-gooders and the politically sensitive; conservative business and financial circles as well have seen the threat to the urban order which such concentrations pose. The threat is not merely one of occasional political agitations by a large non-white group; investments are jeopardized and economic routines disrupted by the social distress of the disadvantaged group.[10] Higher taxes and public insolvency are foreseen and dreaded.

Industry and commercial circles have become increasingly concerned with the problem of housing segregation. Such groups as the Committee for Economic Development, the American Council to Improve Our Neighborhoods and *Fortune*

Magazine have launched programs to make known the strains that continued segregation imposes on the economy of cities. The mortgage banks, the large homebuilders and real estate interests have grasped the long-range meaning of the fair housing practices laws. They may be distressed by such laws, but the political and legal significance is clear. Now tools are being forged to attack racial restrictions. Segregation is going to mean increasing troubles for business.

The intellectual leaders of the cities have long been committed to desegregation. They have often had to sit by wringing their hands, however, because they were excluded from the practical decisions of political and civic life.[11] This situation is slowly changing. The intellectual is gaining more respect as our society matures. The urban universities are entering more deeply into civic concerns. The complexity of urban problems has dictated that the old power and machine politicians have had to make alliances with the intellectual and technical elite. Intergroup agencies and planning commissions now share the responsibility for urban decisions affecting minority groups. The intellectuals have ever more media open to them for the shaping of public opinion.

It appears, then, that both those who hold the purse strings of the cities and those who profess to be expert in its social problems are prepared to rise to a new level of responsibility in coping with racial matters.[12] Despite this good omen, it is not the business and intellectual leaders of the cities who will be the primary force in bringing about residential desegregation and the resulting social readjustments. However much white leadership in these categories may desire readjustment, the central role is not theirs. It is extremely doubtful if these leaders could persuade the very skeptical general white public of the necessity and wisdom of housing desegregation. What is conceded at the upper levels of urban society is not even accorded

a hearing at the local community level, where housing segregation is defended. The leaders who carry the racial confrontation to this level, and into all those corners of urban society
where resentment and misgivings abide, will be those of the
minority itself. The civil rights professionals and sympathetic
religious and civic spokesmen will play an important advisory
and preparatory role, but the ultimate acts of choice and commitment will be those of Negro families and their representatives.

Negro Leadership

It is common for leaders in the civic and social service work
of large cities to bewail the lack of educated and responsible
Negro leadership to help in overcoming the problems of in-
migrants, the culturally deprived and the wayward in the segregated neighborhoods. Every city has had the problem of
scarcity of leadership in each of the successive immigrant
groups. That the complaint is made about Negroes is not notable. Every city has what it believes to be Negro leaders, but
very often the majority group can be quite mistaken about who
is a minority group leader. This is particularly true today, when
sweeping changes are taking place in the leadership elements of
the Negro population in this country. The old minister-turned-
political-leader is now accompanied by a covey of new types.
As the great national issue of race relations takes a new form
in the urban areas, Negro leadership is being revitalized and
transformed as if in preparation for an historic final struggle.[13]

If we analyze the changes overtaking Negro leadership, we
can foresee the ways in which minority approaches to the segregation problem will differ in the future. There is, first of all,
a growth of movements to overcome specific racial barriers.

These movements are often spontaneous, such as the Southern sit-ins or the Montgomery bus boycotts. The rise of such crusades has been part of the Negro tradition in the past, but modern mass media and greater population give them added effects today. They are characterized by a zeal and an inventive enthusiasm that give them a powerful thrust.[14] Their leadership often arises in an impromptu and even an accidental manner, but it is highly attractive and at times charismatic. While it is true that the most vivid demonstration of this kind of movement and its protagonists has been in the South, the impact of its development in the 1950's on the psychology of Northern Negroes has been tremendous. The use of boycott tactics against schools considered to be inferior in Brooklyn and New Rochelle, New York, indicates their appeal to Northern Negroes. The coincidence of a cause, a location and an adored leader for the ignition of wildfire civil rights protest in the Northern cities seems only a matter of time.

Indirectly related to the special civil rights movements has been the development of conscious rebel leadership. Although they may emerge suddenly to prominence, the rebel leaders are self-directed, and their plans are the result of long periods of gestation. The most typical example of the extremist and rebel leadership is that of the Black Muslims. Another example is Robert Williams, the NAACP chapter head in South Carolina who insisted upon arming his supporters against white violence.[15] Paul Zuber, the vociferous lawyer who resigned from the New York NAACP housing committee, is another example of an able, flamboyant protagonist. Such leaders may or may not lead spontaneous movements, but they are formidable in that they have programs which can be swept into execution by sudden waves of enthusiasm.

Another new echelon of Negro leaders are those who have found themselves heads of permanent mass membership organizations. For years such groups as the NAACP and the Urban League were small organizations of dedicated people. In the post-war years publicity, population growth and rising education have swelled the ranks of such groups until the leaders now find themselves the heads of widespread administrative networks. If such leaders are somewhat more conservative than those in the protest movements, they merely reflect the realities of the increased strength of their organizations and the human tendency to use great power cautiously.

Another segment of the new Negro leadership is that which has attained key positions in the general institutions of urban society. Men such as Ralph Bunche, A. Philip Randolph and Robert Weaver have achieved success on their own merits. More and more Negroes are rising to crucial posts in government and civic life in the cities. These men, in their individual way, are as significant as the various movements and organizations. They represent success, acceptance and respect.

This creative phalanx has augmented the old "folk" leaders and ministers in the churches. While these leadership elements represent too broad a front to function in total accord and in simultaneous action, they are united by the motto of "Progress now!" on racial matters. Negro political leadership generally lags behind this front-line segment.

According to James Q. Wilson, who studied Negroes in politics in Chicago, the politician is muzzled by the necessities of keeping his patronage job or by the interests of party harmony.[16] New York's Adam Clayton Powell, a singular personality in any setting, may be an exception pointing the way toward flamboyant exploitation of political advantages in civil rights. With or without the aid of the urban Negro politicians, however, the new leadership elements are intent on demolishing segregation, often without respect to whether this will engender harsh reactions among whites.[17]

Formula for Our Future

Against this background of leadership change, let us consider what general conditions are necessary for a large-scale overturning of the racially restrictive housing pattern in the urban areas.

A first, and perhaps an overriding, consideration is that economic opportunity must continue to be a basis for housing opportunity. It might even be argued that a prosperous economy is a *sine qua non* for housing desegregation. Unless housing is built to replace our obsolescent dwellings, and unless minority families have the buying power to bargain for such housing, talk about desegregation is academic. It is only in an atmosphere of economic advance and optimism that Negroes can hope to buy dwellings on a desegregated basis. The responsibility for the promotion of full employment and adequate housing production rests jointly with the private and public sectors of the economy.

Because of the extent and complexity of housing segregation, mass minority opinion has not yet been effectively marshalled against it. Judging from recent civil rights activity, a mass campaign in housing is manageable and feasible.[18] Such a departure in the urban areas will be the single most effective device for galvanizing white leadership and promoting the education of the suspicious white public. There is no substitute for direct confrontation to provide a basis for serious community consideration of the justice and urgency of desegregation. This confrontation takes desegregation out of the realm of the merely possible and convinces the white public that Negro residential dispersion has to be dealt with here and now. All the preachments and appeals and all of the educational programs are made specific by the arrival of Negroes on the local scene.

This, then, is the second component of a formula for urban freedom of movement that will bring about desegregation: the actual residential movement of Negroes into the restricted sections of the housing market.

There are other factors in the formula that must accompany the residential dispersion of the more capable minority families. One must be the watchful presence of government influence that is committed not only to non-discrimination—the even-handed application of its services—but to a full affirmative policy of desegregation. No government position short of such a policy will bring about unrestricted mobility for minority families; a passive role of tolerating whatever housing desegregation occurs will merely underwrite the status quo. Positive public efforts must be made to overcome the legacy of inertia and privation that handicaps the non-white population in its aspirations for housing improvement. This implies a full range of government concern with economic, legal and educational matters as they affect the housing market.

As part of the government policy of desegregation there must also be crystal-clear guarantees of the full and safe enjoyment of property once it is acquired by non-whites. These guarantees must be made concrete at the local level. A community consensus must be built up which absolutely and unmistakably will not permit conspiracy, intimidation and harassment to bedevil property acquisition by non-whites. This is partly a task for lawyers and law enforcement officials, particularly the police forces, but it is also the responsibility of civic and political leadership.

A further element in the formula for urban action to overcome residential segregation is the work of intergroup relations and civil rights groups. It will not be enough simply for non-whites to move and for government to guard their right to do so. Even under the best of circumstances there are bound to be difficult problems of adjustment that can be handled only by organizations adept at persuasive community education work. The most responsible portions of public opinion must be induced not only to accept racial change, but to monitor it and protect it from the spasms of local excitement that are bound to accompany it in communities consecrated to racial exclusiveness for generations.

The suppositions set forth above do involve the state to a notable degree. This involvement is not premised upon any simple contention that since the state has tacitly condoned segregation in the past, it must affirmatively undo segregation in the future. That would be an over-simplification. The basis of state support for desegregation is the public obligation of the government to secure justice. In a society where the question of racial change is posed on many social levels, ranging over a wide geographical area and over a long period of time, only the pervasive sovereignty of the government can exercise the vigilance necessary to insure minimum guarantees of legality, order and progress when the change occurs. We shall not, because of this government role, fall prey to the delusion that public power can somehow dissolve racism. The ultimate tests will be in human relations at the local level, where the might and majesty of government are clumsy and often fumbling.

There is, indeed, as we have repeatedly pointed out, a danger of political demagoguery in desegregation—as there has been in segregation. Government influence must be wisely used. We are beset by too much bureaucratic and governmental meddling as matters stand today. The use of state power in race relations problems is a condition for a social solution, not the solution itself.

The People's Decisions

Ultimately it is on the informal life of the people themselves that we must rely for the reduction of the prejudices that support housing segregation. It is in the intercourse of common daily events that the reasons deriving from humane and democratic principles will assert themselves. It is in the sphere of friendship and co-operative activity that our people will disabuse their minds of the misunderstandings that have created the racial problem. It will not be easy to insure in urban life the contacts which will produce this necessary social experience. We have no such strong local community life as will provide much opportunity for co-operative activity among neighbors. Our city-dwellers tend to be individualistic and preoccupied with specialized fields of activity. Nevertheless we Americans are an informal people. We do not stand on ceremony. Our urban life is a confluence of men of diverse backgrounds, and even though the local residential community may not provide the initial experiences to overcome segregation, the general society will.[19]

If we concede this general tendency toward a multi-racial society, the mechanics of desegregation are still obscure. The process may take turns and confront obstacles in urban life which we have not considered. The various forms that city life is taking could constitute separate strata with differing potentials for desegregation. The downtown apartment and townhouse set is cosmopolitan and without many of the social characteristics that would retard interracial living. This kind of downtown life has proved very popular among the affluent and has begun to attract people back from the suburbs.[20] The economic differential which has prevented Negro participation in this kind of residential milieu will be erased with the years. The integration of this urbane, fashionable, creative downtown population seems assured.

In the older neighborhoods that surround the downtown area, two developments have been at work. The old white immigrant and ethnic enclaves are dissolving. While this dissolution may produce precious little actual interracial residence, it will at least permit movement, so that the Negro population will have somewhat more flexibility within the central city framework. As we have seen, the native white working class has continued to abandon the central city neighborhoods as the Negro concentrations expanded, and this abandonment has opened up a tolerable supply of housing to take the edge off the worst housing difficulties of non-whites. Public housing and urban renewal projects have assisted in this process. There is a possibility that the Negro population will respond so vigorously to the improved living conditions in the core city that a whole new set of civic standards and achievements will arise within the Negro communities, serving to counteract the attractions of desegregation and suburbia. Most Negroes have never actually experienced desegregation or suburban living anyway. Our urban society does present extraordinary opportunities, and a burst of civic and cultural creativity among Negroes is a real possibility. While such a development might fortify segregated living patterns, it might also enrich our urban life in an exciting way.

The broad reaches of suburbia can probably be affected by a significant dispersion of Negroes in the metropolitan areas, permitting token non-white residence in the outer rings of the metropolitan areas. This representation will be conditioned by the class criteria of suburbia. But the prospect of mass non-white movement to suburbia is not great. Economics, social psychology and mere physical distance militate against such movement—an intermediate residential step appears to be required. The suburbs seem to represent the most serious long-term problem with respect to racial distribution. It is not so much that they are largely free of non-whites today and that this condition is not likely to change markedly over the next decade; much more troublesome is the fact that they are in schism with respect to the rest of the metropolis. This breach will not be easily healed by any of the available means—political, economic or educational. Racially, the cleavage may be so complete that token non-white representation in the suburbs will mean little. The predominantly white suburban world could remain intact, impenetrable by the cosmopolitan influences of the city, still harboring the old prejudices and assumptions about race and racial concentration. Conversely, the heavily Negro population of the cities could remain estranged from suburbia. This would be particularly serious if the suburbs became what some have predicted, the modal and typical residential communities to which most Americans aspire. They would then become an ideal sphere of American life, essentially restrictive in racial outlook, divorced from the vast majority of the country's non-white population.

The metropolitan way of life, with its technical proficiency and physical convenience, is now the dominant type of social life for our citizens. As we have constantly emphasized in this book, this expanding urbanism has grown up with grave defects. Its formative period was under the auspices of an exploitive laissez-faire capitalism which promoted almost as much disorder and social damage as it did solid progress and achievement. The new urbanism, though more disciplined and efficient, has not produced a viable form of responsible, democratic community life in the residential sphere. The civic and cultural development of the metropolis has suffered from the lack of any framework for the integrity of local life. The evolution of leadership has been often interrupted, subject to crude and predatory inroads. As a result of these deficiencies the cities have become disordered and are in financial danger.

Cities of Freedom

There have been terrifying examples within our own lifetime of the pathological excesses to which civilized urban man can lend himself—for example, the manipulation of the passions of the industrial masses by the Nazi and Soviet tyrannies. The multiple effects of the disorders in urban society do not always come to a head in political or moral calamity. More often they inflict their wounds on urban man in a steady, almost stereo-typed and institutional way. The rigors of technology insofar as it demands a mechanical response; the frenetic stimulation produced by so much of the mass media of communication; the atomized and rudely competitive spirit of urban social life—all exact a toll from us. We pay in terms of juvenile delin-quency, personality disorder, disorganization of the family and the residential community.[21] There is a great danger that threat-ens the affluent life of our technical cities: it is that we shall so far routinize and specialize urban living as to maim our human relations. To do so would betray the most sacred values to which American society is heir. The Greek ideal of the rational man, the hallowed Christian concept of the holiness of life and the Western democratic image of the human citizen residing in dignity are all jeopardized by the haste and disorder, the precocity and the practice of expediency in our new urban world.

The racial problem figures in this panorama in a special way. It is, as we have seen, deeply embedded in our social history. It once tore American society apart in fratricidal conflict. Race relations have been involved in some of the most severe challenges posed by the internal competition within American society. In the political sphere, racial factors have been of tremendous import not only with respect to the South, but with respect to national policy regarding frontier settlement, the restriction of immigration and the sharing of social opportunities. In the field of education, racial considerations have compromised the great strides we have made in spreading literacy and conferring new cultural opportunities on the free citizen. No social problem except those of war and the stable organization of the metropolis itself has such meaning for the United States as the racial problem. Whether or not we can achieve racial harmony may be a test of our fidelity to pluralist principles. If we find ourselves unable to desegregate the urban areas to any appreciable degree, we must arrive at some civilized rationale within the pluralist framework for balancing the racial worlds which remain.

If, on the other hand, we can bring about desegregation on a scale which produces genuine broad areas of interracial living, we shall have elevated our society in a vivid and liberating way. We shall have redressed many severe internal inequities. The full potential of all of our people will have been summoned to realization. Our commitment to democracy will no longer be subject to question by those malignant foes who are competing with us for the initiative in a world caught up in social upheavals. Not only shall we have reversed an historic defeat in our social life and culture, but we shall have availed ourselves of the factor of racial difference as a forge of unity. Our cities, so astonishing in their wealth and vitality, will be renewed in freedom. Their inclusiveness and the nobility of the democratic ethic by which they flourish will be assured again in the eyes of the skeptic and the historian. But, above all, we shall have proved to ourselves and to the sons who come after us that the American cities we have built are worthy settings for the exercise of those virtues and ideals which have shone like jewels on the strife-anointed brow of Western man. These are the rewards that await us if we can banish racism from the cities of our land.

NOTES

1. C. Eric Lincoln, *The Black Muslims* (Boston, Beacon Press, 1961).
2. Ashmore, *The Other Side of the Jordan,* p. 111.
3. David Carlson, "The New Urbanites and the City Housing Crisis," *Architectural Forum,* June and July 1960, p. 116.
4. "Negro in Suburbs Facing Problems," *New York Times,* May 21, 1961.
5. "12 Cities' Suburbs Called 93% White," *New York Times,* May 7, 1961.
6. S. Lipset and R. Bendix, *Social Mobility in Industrial Society* (Berkeley, University of California Press, 1959), p. 80.
7. *Ibid.,* p. 80.
8. Louis Wirth, "Racial Segregation in the City," *American Journal of Sociology,* July 1927.
9. Jitsuichi Masurka, "The City and the Race Problem," *American Journal of Sociology,* November 1944, p. 200.
10. Hannah Lees, "The Not-Buying Power of Philadelphia Negroes," *The Reporter,* May 11, 1961. This tells of a shrewdly disguised and successful economic boycott of major corporation products by Negroes seeking greater employment opportunities. Such tactics are typical of what can be expected if Negroes are excluded from the general benefits of urban life.
11. See M. and L. White, "The American Intellectual Versus the American City," *Daedalus,* Winter 1961.
12. See a talk by David Rockefeller, "Urban Renewal: Problem of the Center City," published by Chase Manhattan Bank, 1961.
13. I am indebted to the eminent sociologist Dr. Ira D. Reid for some of the observations on minority leadership here. Similar observations were contained in a lecture given in Philadelphia on April 12, 1961, to the local chapter of the National Association of Intergroup Relations Officials.

14. See James Baldwin, *New York Times Magazine,* March 12, 1961.

15. Julien Mayfield, "Challenge to Negro Leadership," *Commentary,* April 1961.

16. James Q. Wilson, *Negro Politics* (Glencoe, Ill., The Free Press, 1960).

17. Kyle Haselden, *The Racial Problem in Christian Perspective* (New York, Harper, 1959), p. 105. "For many of us, exempt as we are from the stigma of race and free from the harassments of an oppressive social order, the questions of immediacy and gradualism, of coercion and persuasion, may seem academic. But they are not so for the Negro. Experience has for him been a dear teacher. For 246 years he languished in slavery waiting for the heart of Pharoah to be moved; but freedom did not come until Moses went down and told old Pharoah to let his people go. For many years, in response to a persuasive orator and beloved leader, the Negro let down his buckets where he was, but they always brought up a brackish water; and the water was not sweetened until he began to draw from a different and truly 'mighty stream.' For decades he waited at the white man's door, hat in hand; but he has learned that for him there is much more to be gained by standing at the front holding, not a hat, but a subpoena. So thoroughly is the leadership of the Negro race and most of its followers converted to this new strategy that they will not be persuaded to wait with their long hopes until there are enough men of good will to make those hopes a reality. They have measured the results of decades of waiting against the results of brief years of acting; and they no longer have a choice."

18. Negroes can challenge the segregation practices in the South under highly dangerous conditions; it seems only a question of time and tactics until devices are found for challenging segregated housing. Sit-ins and stand-ins at rental offices and sample houses may be a foretaste. The Congress on Racial Equality is experimenting with such tactics.

19. Sociologist Georg Simmel long ago pointed out that in our kind of society the deficiencies of smaller or specialized groups or locales can be made up by a "higher organic synthesis" of opinion and experience. See Georg Simmel, *Conflict and the Web of Group Affiliations* (Glencoe, Ill., The Free Press, 1955), p. 195.

20. See The Editors of Fortune Magazine, *The Exploding Metropolis.*

21. Such books as J. L. Sert, *Can Our Cities Survive?* (Cambridge,

Harvard University Press, 1942), David Riesman, *The Lonely Crowd,* and J. Ortega y Gasset, *The Revolt of the Masses* (New York, Norton, 1932), depict these urban pathologies.